Mediterranean Refresh Cookbook

1200-Day Quick, Delicious and Healthy Fresh Recipes for Living and Eating Well Every Day

Kalistin Gasamy

Table of Contents

INTRODUCTION

What is the definition of Mediterranean Refresh Diet?

The Mediterranean Refresh Diet is a dietary approach that draws inspiration from the traditional Mediterranean diet while incorporating some modern elements. It emphasizes the consumption of fresh, whole foods, particularly fruits, vegetables, whole grains, legumes, nuts, and seeds. The diet encourages the use of olive oil as the primary source of fat, moderate consumption of fish and poultry, and limited intake of red meat. It also promotes the inclusion of dairy products, such as yogurt and cheese, in moderation.

The Mediterranean Refresh Diet places a strong emphasis on plant-based foods, which provide a wide range of nutrients, antioxidants, and fiber. It encourages the consumption of seasonal and locally sourced produce to maximize freshness and flavor. The diet also encourages individuals to reduce their intake of processed foods, refined grains, added sugars, and unhealthy fats.

In addition to the food choices, the Mediterranean Refresh Diet emphasizes mindful eating, enjoying meals with family and friends, and being physically active. It recognizes the importance of lifestyle factors, such as regular physical activity, stress management, and adequate sleep, in promoting overall health and well-being.

Overall, the Mediterranean Refresh Diet is a balanced and sustainable approach to eating that has been associated with numerous health benefits, including reduced risk of heart disease, improved weight management, and better overall health outcomes.

How does the Mediterranean Refresh Diet differ from other Mediterranean diets?

The Mediterranean Refresh Diet is a modern adaptation of the traditional Mediterranean diet, incorporating some modifications and updates to align with current nutritional guidelines and preferences. While it shares many similarities with other Mediterranean diets, there are a few key differences that set it apart. In this response, I will elaborate on these differences and explain how the Mediterranean Refresh Diet differs from other Mediterranean diets.

- Emphasis on Fresh and Seasonal Foods: One distinctive feature of the Mediterranean Refresh Diet is the emphasis on fresh, seasonal foods. It encourages individuals to consume locally sourced produce that is in season, maximizing freshness, flavor, and nutritional value. This approach promotes a closer connection to nature, supports local agriculture, and ensures a diverse and varied diet throughout the year. By prioritizing fresh foods, the Mediterranean Refresh Diet aims to provide optimal nutrition while promoting sustainability and environmental consciousness.

- Reduced Red Meat Consumption: While the traditional Mediterranean diet includes moderate consumption of red meat, the Mediterranean Refresh Diet suggests limiting its intake. Red meat is often replaced with leaner protein sources such as fish and poultry. This modification aligns with current dietary recommendations that advocate for reducing red meat consumption due to its association with an increased risk of certain health conditions, including cardiovascular disease and certain types of cancer. By reducing red meat intake, the Mediterranean Refresh Diet promotes a healthier protein balance and encourages individuals to explore alternative protein sources.

- Inclusion of Plant-Based Proteins: Another notable difference in the Mediterranean Refresh Diet is the increased emphasis on plant-based proteins. While the traditional Mediterranean diet includes legumes as a protein source, the Mediterranean Refresh Diet expands the variety of plant-based proteins to include a wider range of options such as tofu, tempeh, and plant-based meat substitutes. This modification caters to individuals who follow vegetarian or vegan lifestyles or those who prefer to reduce their reliance on animal-based proteins. By incorporating more plant-based proteins, the Mediterranean Refresh Diet offers a diverse and flexible approach to meeting protein needs while promoting sustainability and reducing the environmental impact associated with animal agriculture.

- Mindful Eating and Lifestyle Factors: The Mediterranean Refresh Diet recognizes the importance of mindful eating and lifestyle factors in promoting overall health and well-being. It emphasizes the enjoyment of meals, encourages individuals to savor and appreciate the flavors of food, and promotes mindful eating practices such as eating slowly and paying attention to hunger and fullness cues. Additionally, the diet highlights the significance of regular physical activity, stress management, and adequate sleep as integral components of a healthy lifestyle. By incorporating these lifestyle factors, the Mediterranean Refresh Diet aims to support not only physical health but also mental and emotional well-being.

- Adaptation to Modern Preferences and Convenience: The Mediterranean Refresh Diet acknowledges the realities of modern life and the need for convenience. It offers practical suggestions and adaptations to make the diet more accessible and feasible for individuals with busy schedules. This may include providing tips for meal planning, batch cooking, and incorporating time-saving techniques without compromising the nutritional integrity of the diet. By addressing the challenges of modern lifestyles, the Mediterranean Refresh Diet aims to make healthy eating more attainable and sustainable for a wider range of individuals.

In summary, the Mediterranean Refresh Diet is a modern interpretation of the traditional Mediterranean diet that incorporates fresh, seasonal foods, reduces red meat consumption, includes a variety of plant-based proteins, emphasizes mindful eating and lifestyle factors, and adapts to modern preferences and convenience. While it shares the core principles of the Mediterranean diet, the Mediterranean Refresh Diet offers a contemporary approach that aligns with current nutritional guidelines and addresses the evolving needs and preferences of individuals.

What are some of the benefits and challenges of following the Mediterranean Refresh Diet?

Following the Mediterranean Refresh Diet can offer numerous benefits for overall health and well-being. However, like any dietary approach, there may also be some challenges to consider. In this response, I will discuss the benefits and challenges of following the Mediterranean Refresh Diet.

Benefits of the Mediterranean Refresh Diet:

- Reduced Risk of Chronic Diseases: The Mediterranean Refresh Diet has been associated with a reduced risk of various chronic diseases, including heart disease, type 2 diabetes, certain types of cancer, and neurodegenerative conditions like Alzheimer's disease. This is attributed to the diet's emphasis on whole, nutrient-dense foods, such as fruits, vegetables, whole grains, and healthy fats like olive oil, which provide a wide range of antioxidants, vitamins, minerals, and fiber.

- Heart-Healthy Effects: The Mediterranean Refresh Diet is known for its heart-healthy effects. It promotes the consumption of foods that are rich in monounsaturated fats, such as olive oil, which can help improve cholesterol levels and reduce the risk of cardiovascular disease. The diet also includes omega-3 fatty acids from fish, which have been shown to have protective effects on heart health.

- Weight Management: The Mediterranean Refresh Diet is not a weight-loss diet per se, but it can support healthy weight management. The diet emphasizes whole, unprocessed foods that are naturally lower in calories and higher in fiber, promoting satiety and reducing the likelihood of overeating. Additionally, the diet encourages regular physical activity, which is crucial for maintaining a healthy weight.

- Improved Cognitive Function: The Mediterranean Refresh Diet has been linked to improved cognitive function and a reduced risk of cognitive decline. The diet's emphasis on antioxidant-rich foods, healthy fats, and nutrients like B vitamins and omega-3 fatty acids may contribute to better brain health and cognitive performance.

- Enhanced Gut Health: The Mediterranean Refresh Diet is rich in fiber from fruits, vegetables, whole grains, and legumes. This dietary fiber serves as a prebiotic, nourishing the beneficial bacteria in the gut and promoting a healthy gut microbiome. A balanced and diverse gut microbiome is associated with various health benefits, including improved digestion, enhanced immune function, and reduced inflammation.

Challenges of the Mediterranean Refresh Diet:

- Availability and Cost: Depending on the region and access to fresh, seasonal produce, following the Mediterranean Refresh Diet may pose challenges in terms of availability and cost. Some individuals may have limited access to fresh, local produce or find it more expensive compared to processed or convenience foods. However, with proper planning and exploring local markets, it is possible to find affordable options and adapt the diet to suit different budgets.

- Cultural and Culinary Preferences: The Mediterranean Refresh Diet is based on the traditional dietary patterns of Mediterranean countries, which may differ from individual cultural and culinary preferences. Adapting to new flavors and cooking techniques can be a challenge for some individuals. However, the Mediterranean Refresh Diet allows for flexibility and encourages individuals to incorporate their cultural preferences and adapt the diet to their taste while still adhering to the core principles.

- Social Situations and Eating Out: Following any specific diet can be challenging in social situations or when eating out. The Mediterranean Refresh Diet may require some adjustments and choices when dining at restaurants or attending social gatherings where the available options may not align perfectly with the diet's recommendations. However, most restaurants offer Mediterranean-inspired dishes, and with mindful choices, it is possible to make healthier selections while still enjoying social occasions.

- Learning New Cooking Techniques: The Mediterranean Refresh Diet encourages home cooking and the use of fresh ingredients. For individuals who are not accustomed to cooking or are unfamiliar with Mediterranean cuisine, learning new cooking techniques and recipes may require some effort and time. However, there are numerous resources available, such as cookbooks, online recipes, and cooking classes, to help individuals explore and learn new culinary skills.

- Individual Preferences and Allergies: Like any dietary approach, the Mediterranean Refresh Diet may not suit everyone's individual preferences or dietary restrictions. For example, individuals with specific food allergies or intolerances may need to make modifications to accommodate their needs. However, the diet's flexibility allows for customization and adaptation to individual preferences and requirements.

In conclusion, the Mediterranean Refresh Diet offers several benefits for overall health and well-being, including reduced risk of chronic diseases, heart-healthy effects, weight management support, improved cognitive function, and enhanced gut health. While there may be challenges associated with availability and cost, cultural preferences, social situations, learning new cooking techniques, and individual dietary restrictions, these challenges can be overcome with proper planning, flexibility, and adaptation. Overall, the Mediterranean Refresh Diet provides a balanced and sustainable approach to eating that can be tailored to individual needs and preferences.

How can you incorporate the Mediterranean Refresh Diet into your daily life?

Incorporating the Mediterranean Refresh Diet into your daily life can be a rewarding and enjoyable experience. By following a few key principles and making conscious choices, you can embrace this dietary approach and reap its benefits. Here are some practical tips to help you incorporate the Mediterranean Refresh Diet into your daily routine:

- Prioritize Plant-Based Foods: The Mediterranean Refresh Diet places a strong emphasis on plant-based foods such as fruits, vegetables, whole grains, legumes, nuts, and seeds. Make sure to include these foods in every meal. Aim for a variety of colorful fruits and vegetables to maximize nutrient intake. Include whole grains like quinoa, brown rice, and whole wheat bread in your meals. Experiment with different legumes such as chickpeas, lentils, and black beans. Snack on nuts and seeds for a healthy dose of fats and protein.

- Choose Healthy Fats: Healthy fats are an essential component of the Mediterranean Refresh Diet. Opt for sources like olive oil, avocados, and nuts. Use olive oil as your primary cooking oil and salad dressing. Add sliced avocado to your salads, sandwiches, or smoothies. Enjoy a handful of nuts as a snack or sprinkle them on top of your meals for added crunch and flavor.

- Include Fish and Seafood: Fish and seafood are important protein sources in the Mediterranean Refresh Diet. Aim to include fish in your diet at least twice a week. Opt for fatty fish like salmon, mackerel, and sardines, which are rich in omega-3 fatty acids. Grill, bake, or steam fish to retain its nutritional value. If you follow a vegetarian or vegan lifestyle, consider incorporating plant-based sources of omega-3 fatty acids such as flaxseeds, chia seeds, and walnuts.

- Limit Red Meat and Processed Foods: While the Mediterranean Refresh Diet allows for moderate consumption of red meat, it's recommended to limit its intake. Instead, focus on lean protein sources like poultry, eggs, and legumes. Reduce your consumption of processed foods like deli meats, sausages, and packaged snacks, as they are often high in unhealthy fats, sodium, and additives.

- Enjoy Dairy and Dairy Alternatives: The Mediterranean Refresh Diet includes moderate amounts of dairy products like yogurt and cheese. Opt for Greek yogurt, which is high in protein and lower in sugar compared to other varieties. If you prefer dairy alternatives, choose options like almond milk, soy milk, or oat milk. Look for unsweetened varieties to avoid added sugars.

- Embrace Fresh Herbs and Spices: Fresh herbs and spices are essential in Mediterranean cuisine, adding flavor and aroma to dishes. Experiment with herbs like basil, parsley, cilantro, and mint. Use spices such as oregano, thyme, cumin, and paprika to enhance the taste of your meals. Fresh herbs can be added to salads, soups, or used as a garnish, while spices can be incorporated into marinades, dressings, or sauces.

- Make Meals Social and Enjoyable: In Mediterranean cultures, meals are often seen as a social activity to be enjoyed with family and friends. Take the time to savor your meals and eat mindfully. Sit down at a table, turn off distractions, and focus on the flavors and textures of your food. Engage in conversation and enjoy the company of others.

- Engage in Regular Physical Activity: The Mediterranean Refresh Diet recognizes the importance of physical activity for overall health and well-being. Incorporate regular exercise into your daily routine. Choose activities that you enjoy, whether it's walking, cycling, swimming, dancing, or practicing yoga. Aim for at least 150 minutes of moderate-intensity exercise or 75 minutes of vigorous exercise per week.

- Plan and Prepare Meals in Advance: Planning and preparing meals in advance can help you stay on track with the Mediterranean Refresh Diet. Set aside time each week to plan your meals, create a shopping list, and prepare ingredients in advance. Batch cook and store meals in portioned containers for easy grab-and-go options during busy days.

- **Explore Mediterranean-Inspired Recipes:** There are countless Mediterranean-inspired recipes available that can help you diversify your meals and keep things interesting. Look for cookbooks, online recipe websites, or cooking apps that specialize in Mediterranean cuisine. Try new recipes and experiment with different flavors and ingredients to find your favorites.

Remember, the Mediterranean Refresh Diet is not about strict rules or deprivation but rather about embracing a balanced and sustainable approach to eating. It's important to listen to your body, honor your individual preferences, and make choices that align with your unique needs and lifestyle. By incorporating these tips into your daily life, you can embrace the Mediterranean Refresh Diet and enjoy its numerous health benefits.

What are the main foods and ingredients of the Mediterranean Refresh Diet?

The Mediterranean Refresh Diet is characterized by a wide variety of wholesome and nutrient-dense foods. Here are some of the main foods and ingredients that are typically included in this dietary approach:

- **Fruits and Vegetables:** The Mediterranean Refresh Diet emphasizes the consumption of a wide range of fruits and vegetables. These include tomatoes, cucumbers, bell peppers, spinach, kale, broccoli, zucchini, eggplant, citrus fruits, berries, melons, and more. These colorful and fiber-rich foods provide essential vitamins, minerals, antioxidants, and phytochemicals.

- **Whole Grains:** Whole grains are an important component of the Mediterranean Refresh Diet. Examples include whole wheat, brown rice, quinoa, oats, barley, and bulgur. These grains are rich in fiber, B vitamins, and minerals. They provide sustained energy and contribute to a feeling of fullness.

- **Legumes:** Legumes, such as chickpeas, lentils, beans, and peas, are a staple in the Mediterranean Refresh Diet. They are excellent sources of plant-based protein, fiber, and complex carbohydrates. Legumes can be used in soups, stews, salads, and side dishes.

- **Healthy Fats:** Healthy fats, particularly monounsaturated fats, are prominent in the Mediterranean Refresh Diet. Olive oil is the primary source of fat and is used for cooking, dressing salads, and drizzling over dishes. Other sources of healthy fats include avocados, nuts (such as almonds, walnuts, and pistachios), and seeds (such as flaxseeds, chia seeds, and sesame seeds).

- Fish and Seafood: Fish and seafood are important sources of protein and omega-3 fatty acids in the Mediterranean Refresh Diet. Fatty fish like salmon, mackerel, sardines, and trout are particularly rich in omega-3s. These nutrients have been associated with numerous health benefits, including heart health and brain function.

- Poultry, Eggs, and Dairy: Poultry, such as chicken and turkey, is consumed in moderation in the Mediterranean Refresh Diet. Eggs are also included as a source of protein and nutrients. Dairy products, such as Greek yogurt and cheese, are enjoyed in moderation. These foods provide calcium, protein, and other essential nutrients.

- Herbs and Spices: Fresh herbs and spices are used abundantly in Mediterranean cuisine to enhance flavors without relying on excessive salt. Common herbs include basil, parsley, mint, oregano, thyme, and rosemary. Spices like garlic, cumin, paprika, cinnamon, and turmeric add depth and complexity to dishes.

- Nuts and Seeds: Nuts and seeds are often consumed as snacks or used as toppings in Mediterranean dishes. They provide a good source of healthy fats, protein, fiber, and essential minerals. Almonds, walnuts, pistachios, flaxseeds, chia seeds, and sesame seeds are commonly used.

- Fresh and Dried Fruits: Fresh fruits are enjoyed as snacks or desserts in the Mediterranean Refresh Diet. Dried fruits, such as dates, figs, and raisins, are used in moderation to add natural sweetness to dishes.

- Red Wine (in moderation): Red wine, in moderation, is a traditional part of the Mediterranean diet. It is typically consumed with meals and is believed to have some health benefits due to its antioxidant content. However, it's important to note that excessive alcohol consumption can have negative effects on health, so moderation is key.

These are just some of the main foods and ingredients that make up the Mediterranean Refresh Diet. The diet encourages a wide variety of whole, unprocessed foods, with an emphasis on plant-based ingredients, healthy fats, and lean proteins. It promotes a balanced and enjoyable approach to eating that can contribute to overall health and well-being.

Chapter 1: Breakfast

Loaded Mediterranean Omelette

Prep Time: 10 Minutes   Cook Time: 2 Minutes   Serves: 2

Ingredients:

- 4 large eggs
- 2 tbsp fat-free milk
- 1/4 tsp baking powder (optional)
- 1/2 tsp Spanish paprika
- 1/4 tsp ground allspice
- Salt and pepper, to your liking (I used about 1/2 tsp each)
- 1 1/2 tsp Private Reserve Greek extra virgin olive oil
- 1 tzatziki sauce recipe to serve, optional
- Warm pita to serve, optional
- oppings
- 1/2 cup cherry tomatoes, halved
- 2 tbsp sliced pitted Kalamata olives
- 1/4 to 1/3 cup marinated artichoke hearts, drained and quartered
- 2 tbsp chopped fresh parsley, more for later
- 2 tbsp chopped fresh mint, more for later
- Crumbled feta cheese, to your liking, optional

Directions:

1. In a mixing bowl, add the eggs, milk, baking powder (if using), spices, salt and pepper. Quickly and vigorously whisk to combine.
2. In a 10-inch non-stick skillet, heat extra virgin olive oil until shimmering but not smoking. Be sure to tilt the skillet to coat the bottom well with oil.
3. Pour the egg mixture in and immediately stir with a heat-resistant spatula for like 5 seconds. Then push the cooked portions at the edge toward the center, tilting the pan to allow uncooked egg to fill in around the edges. When no more egg runs to the sides, continue to cook until almost set and the bottom is light golden (about 1 minute.) Remember, the omelette has more time to cook once filled and folded.
4. Remove the skillet from the heat. Spoon a good portion of the toppings onto the center third of the omelette. Use the spatula to fold. Add the remainder of the toppings on top. Sprinkle a little more fresh herbs.
5. Slice the omelette into two halves and serve hot. If you like, add a side of Greek tzatziki sauce and warm pita bread. Enjoy!

Nutritional Value (Amount per Serving):

Calories: 166; Fat: 12.59; Carb: 6.35; Protein: 7.03

Pomegranate Tomato Salad Recipe

Prep Time: 10 Minutes   Cook Time: 0 Minute   Serves: 6

Ingredients:

- 5 tomatoes on the vine, diced very small (about 3 packed cups of small diced tomatoes)
- 1 green bell pepper, cored and chopped
- 2 shallots, finely chopped
- Seeds (arils) of 2 pomegranates
- 10-15 fresh mint leaves, torn
- Salt
- or Dressing
- 2 garlic cloves, minced
- 1/4 cup Private Reserve or Early Harvest Greek extra virgin olive oil
- 2 tbsp white wine vinegar
- 2 tbsp pomegranate juice
- 3/4 tsp ground allspice
- 1/2 tsp ground sumac

Directions:

1. Place the chopped tomatoes in a colander fitted on top of a bowl for 15 minutes or so. This is an optional step, but will help drain a bit of the tomato juice.
2. In a salad bowl, add the chopped tomatoes with the remaining salad ingredients. Season with salt. Mix gently.
3. In a small bowl or mason jar, mix the dressing ingredients.
4. Pour the dressing over the salad and mix to combine. Enjoy!

Nutritional Value (Amount per Serving):

Calories: 193; Fat: 6.82; Carb: 28.93; Protein: 9.64

Eggs With Summer Tomatoes, Zucchini, And Bell Peppers

Prep Time: 10 Minutes   Cook Time: 38 Minutes   Serves: 2

Ingredients:

- 1 tablespoon olive oil
- 1 small yellow onion, halved and thinly sliced
- 1 clove garlic, minced
- 2 medium summer squash or zucchini (approximately 4 cups)
- 2 medium tomatoes, chopped (approximately 3 cups)
- 1/2 teaspoon fresh thyme
- (optional)
- 1 teaspoon ground Spanish piquillo pepper or Spanish paprika
- 1 medium red bell pepper (see Recipe Note)
- Salt and pepper
- 2 large eggs

Directions:

1. Heat the olive oil in a large, heavy skillet over medium heat. Add the onion and cook, stirring often, until translucent, about 5 minutes. Add the garlic and cook for another minute. Add squash and cook until it begins to soften and brown, about 10 minutes. Add the tomatoes, thyme (if using), and

piquillo or paprika, and let simmer until everything is cooked down thick and stewy, about 20 minutes.

2. While the ratatouille is cooking, roast the pepper on the stovetop; see How To Roast Peppers on the Stovetop. Once it has cooled, remove the core and seeds, and cut into 1-inch pieces. Remove the skillet from the heat, add the roasted peppers, and salt and pepper to taste. Let the dish cool before serving — it's best served warm or at room temperature.

3. Fry the eggs (see how here), or prepare them however you prefer. Divide the vegetables between two plates, and top with the eggs. Serve with buttered toast.

Nutritional Value (Amount per Serving):

Calories: 223; Fat: 12.48; Carb: 23.25; Protein: 8.02

Vegan Chickpea Tacos

Prep Time: 10 Minutes   Cook Time: 10 Minutes   Serves: 8

Ingredients:

- 1 tablespoon avocado oil
- 2 (15 oz.) cans chickpeas, drained and rinsed
- 1 teaspoon ground cumin
- 1 teaspoon chili powder
- 1/2 teaspoon paprika
- 1/2 teaspoon garlic powder
- 1/2 teaspoon dried oregano (or Italian seasoning)
- 1 tablespoon soy sauce
- 1/2 teaspoon salt (or to taste)
- 1/4 teaspoon ground black pepper

- (or to taste)
- or Serving:
- 1 cup guacamole
- 1 cup corn, canned or cooked from frozen
- 8 small soft tortillas
- 1/4 cup fresh cilantro, finely chopped
- 1/4 cup sour cream or lime crema (optional)
- 1 lime, wedged

Directions:

Make The Chickpea Filling:

1. Heat oil in a large skillet for 2 minutes over medium-high heat until the hot oil sizzles. Add chickpeas and stir well to cook evenly until golden, about 5 minutes.

2. Add all seasoning including cumin, chili powder, paprika, garlic powder, oregano, soy sauce, salt and pepper. Stir and sauté until evenly coated, about 2-3 minutes. Remove from heat and set aside.

Assemble The Tacos:

1. Heat the soft flour tortillas according to the package instructions, or heat in an ungreased skillet over medium-high heat for 30 seconds per side. You

can also heat it directly on a gas burner for a few seconds to get char marks on the edges

2. Add 2-3 tablespoons chickpeas on each tortilla and top with corn, guacamole and cilantro. Add a dollop of sour cream or lime crema, and squeeze of lime juice, if desired.

Nutritional Value (Amount per Serving):

Calories: 386; Fat: 12.74; Carb: 58.55; Protein: 11.56

Loaded Western Keto Omelette Keto Omelette

Prep Time: 5 Minutes   Cook Time: 5 Minutes   Serves: 1

Ingredients:

- 4 eggs
- 2 strips of bacon (crumbled)
- 1 tablespoon heavy cream
- 1/4 cup green bell pepper (finely chopped)
- 2 tablespoons onion (finely chopped)
- 1/4 cup cheddar cheese
- 2 teaspoons butter or ghee
- 1/4 teaspoon salt
- Pinch of pepper
- Optional Toppings- avocado, salsa, sour cream, cilantro, chives, parsley

Directions:

1. Heat a large skillet over low-medium heat. Add 1 teaspoon of the butter or ghee to the pan and saute onions and peppers until they are slightly tender. Remove onions and peppers from heat. Reduce flame to low.
2. While vegetables are cooking add eggs, heavy cream, salt, and pepper to a large bowl. Whisk for 1 minute until light and fluffy.
3. Add remaining butter to the pan and pour in the egg mixture, tilting the pan to spread into an even layer. When the bottom of the eggs are set and the top is slightly runny, add the vegetables, cheese, and crumbled bacon to one side of the egg circle. Carefully slide the omelette onto a plate, folding over to a half circle.

Nutritional Value (Amount per Serving):

Calories: 1030; Fat: 84.43; Carb: 30.02; Protein: 43.4

Spinach Feta Egg Wrap

Prep Time: 10 Minutes   Cook Time: 5 Minutes   Serves: 1

Ingredients:

- 1 large whole-wheat tortilla
- 1 ½ teaspoons coconut oil

- 1 cup chopped baby spinach leaves
- 1 oil-packed sun-dried tomato, chopped
- 2 eggs, beaten
- ⅓cup feta cheese
- 1 tomato, diced

Directions:

1. Warm tortilla in a large skillet over medium heat.
2. Melt coconut oil in a separate skillet over medium-high heat. Sauté spinach and tomato in hot oil until spinach wilts, about 1 minute. Add eggs and scramble until almost set, about 2 minutes. Sprinkle feta cheese over eggs and continue cooking until cheese melts, about 1 minute more.
3. Transfer scrambled egg mixture to warm tortilla in the large skillet; top with diced tomato. Roll tortilla and leave in skillet long enough for wrap to hold its shape, about 30 seconds.

Nutritional Value (Amount per Serving):

Calories: 649; Fat: 42.17; Carb: 34.92; Protein: 35.87

Make-Ahead Spinach And Feta Egg Casserole

Prep Time: 15 Minutes   Cook Time: 50 Minutes   Serves: 8

Ingredients:

- 1 tablespoon olive oil, plus more for the baking dish
- 1/2 medium yellow onion, diced
- 1/2 medium red bell pepper, cored, seeded, and diced
- 1 1/2 teaspoons kosher salt, divided
- 6 ounces baby spinach (about 6 cups packed), or 8 ounces frozen spinach, thawed, drained, and
- pressed well to remove liquid
- 2 cloves garlic, minced
- 2 tablespoons chopped fresh dill
- 12 large eggs
- 2 cups whole or 2% milk
- 1 tablespoon Dijon mustard
- 1/4 teaspoon freshly ground black pepper
- 4 ounces feta cheese, crumbled (about 1 cup)

Directions:

1. Arrange a rack in the middle of the oven and heat to 375°F. Coat a 9x13-inch baking dish with olive oil.
2. Heat the oil in a large frying pan over medium heat until shimmering. Add the onion, pepper, and 1/2 teaspoon of the salt. Cook, stirring occasionally, until softened, about 5 minutes. Add the spinach and garlic, and toss until wilted and almost all of the liquid is evaporated, about 3 minutes. Remove from the heat and stir in the dill. Transfer to the baking dish and spread in an even layer.

3. Place the eggs, milk, mustard, remaining 1 teaspoon salt, and pepper in a large bowl and whisk until the eggs are completely broken up and incorporated. Pour over the spinach mixture in the baking dish. Sprinkle evenly with the feta.
4. Bake until the top is light golden-brown and a knife inserted in the middle comes out clean, 40 to 45 minutes. Let cool for 5 minutes before slicing.

Nutritional Value (Amount per Serving):

Calories: 236; Fat: 15.77; Carb: 12.53; Protein: 11.55

Whipped Yogurt With Apples And Walnuts

Prep Time: 10 Minutes   Cook Time: 10 Minutes   Serves: 4

Ingredients:
- 1 cup plain Greek yogurt
- 1/2 cup heavy cream
- 1 tablespoon honey
- 2 tablespoons unsalted butter
- 2 firm apples, cored and chopped
- into small 1/2-inch cubes
- 2 tablespoons sugar
- 1/8 teaspoon ground cinnamon
- 1/4 cup walnut halves, toasted and coarsely chopped

Directions:
1. Combine the yogurt, cream, and honey in a bowl, and beat vigorously with a hand mixer until the mixture thickens and forms soft peaks. (You can also use a stand mixer, or whip by hand using a whisk.)
2. Warm the butter in a large skillet over medium heat. Add the apples and 1 tablespoon sugar to the pan. Stir well and cook the apples for 6 to 8 minutes, stirring occasionally to avoid sticking, until they just begin to soften. Once softened, sprinkle the apples with the remaining sugar and the cinnamon, and cook for an additional 2 to 3 minutes. Remove from the heat and let sit for 5 minutes to cool slightly.
3. To serve, spoon a generous serving of whipped yogurt into each bowl and top with warm apples and toasted walnuts.

Nutritional Value (Amount per Serving):

Calories: 227; Fat: 14.97; Carb: 22.62; Protein: 3.64

Bacon, Potato Egg Breakfast Casserole

Prep Time: 5 Minutes   Cook Time: 45 Minutes   Serves: 6

Ingredients:
- Cooking spray or olive oil

- 4 slices thick-cut bacon, cut crosswise into 1/2-inch pieces
- 1 large yellow onion, peeled and diced
- 1 medium yellow bell pepper, diced
- 4 cloves garlic, minced
- 1/3 cup sun-dried tomatoes, chopped
- 2 teaspoons kosher salt, divided
- 8 large eggs
- 1 cup milk (not nonfat)
- 1 teaspoon freshly ground black pepper
- 3 cups frozen diced potatoes (do not thaw)
- 2 cups shredded cheddar cheese

Directions:

1. Arrange a rack in the middle of the oven and heat to 350°F. Coat a 9x13-inch baking dish with baking spray or olive oil; set aside.
2. Place the bacon in a large skillet over medium heat and cook, stirring occasionally, until browned and crisp. Add the onion, bell pepper, garlic, sun-dried tomatoes, and 1 teaspoon of the salt. Cook until the vegetables are fragrant and soft — about 5 minutes more. Remove from the heat and set aside to cool slightly.
3. Place the eggs, milk, remaining 1 teaspoon salt, and pepper in a large bowl and whisk to combine. Stir in the frozen potatoes, cheese, and the bacon-vegetable mixture. (Don't worry; the frozen potatoes cook just fine!) Pour into the prepared baking dish.
4. Bake uncovered until a knife inserted in the center comes out clean and the top is light golden-brown, about 40 minutes. Serve immediately.

Nutritional Value (Amount per Serving):

Calories: 445; Fat: 27.52; Carb: 24.97; Protein: 24.55

Breakfast Grain Salad With Blueberries, Hazelnuts Lemon

Prep Time: 5 Minutes   Cook Time: 20 Minutes   Serves: 8

Ingredients:

- 1 cup steel-cut oats
- 1 cup dry golden quinoa
- 1/2 cup dry millet
- 3 tablespoons olive oil, divided
- 1 (1-inch) piece fresh ginger, peeled and cut into coins
- 2 large lemons, zest and juice
- 1/2 cup maple syrup
- 1 cup Greek yogurt (or soy yogurt, if you want to make this vegan)
- 1/4 teaspoon nutmeg
- 2 cups hazelnuts, roughly chopped and toasted
- 2 cups blueberries or mixed berries

Directions:

1. Mix the oats, quinoa, and millet in a fine mesh strainer and rinse for about

a minute under running water. Set aside.

2. Heat 1 tablespoon olive oil in a 3-quart saucepan over medium-high heat. Add the rinsed grains and cook for 2 to 3 minutes or until they begin smelling toasted. Pour in 4 1/2 cups water and stir in 3/4 teaspoon salt, the ginger coins, and the zest of 1 lemon.

3. Bring to boil, cover, turn down the heat, and simmer for 20 minutes. Turn off the heat and let sit for 5 minutes, then remove the lid and fluff with a fork. Remove the ginger. Spread hot grains on a large baking sheet and let cool for at least half an hour.

4. Spoon the cooled grains into a large bowl. Stir in the zest of the second lemon.

5. In a medium bowl, whisk the remaining 2 tablespoons olive oil with the juice of both lemons until emulsified. Whisk in the maple syrup, yogurt, and nutmeg. Pour this into the grains and stir until well-coated. Stir in the toasted hazelnuts and blueberries. Taste and season with additional salt, if necessary.

6. Refrigerate overnight; the flavors of this really come together overnight in the fridge.

Nutritional Value (Amount per Serving):

Calories: 555; Fat: 28.66; Carb: 71.4; Protein: 13.02

Breakfast Pitas with Chicken Sausage

Prep Time: 10 Minutes   Cook Time: 5 Minutes   Serves: 2

Ingredients:

- 2 pita breads
- 1 tablespoon + 1 teaspoon olive oil separated
- 4 slices mozzarella cheese
- 1 package Jones Dairy Farm All Natural Golden Brown Chicken Breakfast Sausage Patties

- 2 large eggs
- Salt and pepper
- 3/4 cup packed arugula or baby spinach
- 1 avocado
- 1 lemon
- Salt and pepper

Directions:

1. Heat up the grill pan over medium high heat. Brush each side of each pita with 1/2 teaspoon olive oil.
2. Grill 1-2 minutes on each side until slightly crisp.
3. Remove from the grill and allow to slightly cool.
4. Place 2 slices mozzarella cheese on each pita.
5. Prepare the sausage in the microwave according to package directions.

Place 2 sausages on top of each slice of mozzarella cheese.

6. In a large skillet, add remaining 1 tablespoon olive oil over medium high heat. Crack the eggs directly into the pan and cook until the egg whites are set, about 2-3 minutes.
7. Place one egg on top of the chicken sausages on each pita.
8. Divide the arugula or spinach evenly between the two pitas.
9. Slice the avocado and squeeze fresh lemon juice over the avocado.
10. Place the sliced avocado over the spinach or on the side of each plate.
11. Season with a pinch of salt and pepper and enjoy immediately.

Nutritional Value (Amount per Serving):

Calories: 535; Fat: 33.16; Carb: 34.58; Protein: 28.5

Fried Chickpeas And Scrambled Eggs With Garlicky Greens And Spicy Yogurt Recipe

Prep Time: 5 Minutes   Cook Time: 10 Minutes   Serves: 4

Ingredients:

- 2 (14-ounce) cans chickpeas, drained and rinsed
- 2 teaspoons coriander seeds
- 2 teaspoons cumin seeds
- 2 teaspoons flaky sea salt
- 1/2 teaspoon red pepper flakes
- 1 cup plain Greek yogurt
- 3 garlic cloves, 1 minced or finely grated and 2 thinly sliced
- Kosher salt
- 4 tablespoons extra-virgin olive oil
- 6 large eggs, beaten
- 6 scallions, thinly sliced
- 5 ounces (5 cups) baby kale or spinach, coarsely chopped
- 1/2 cup cilantro leaves and tender stems
- Lime wedges, for serving

Directions:

1. Dry the drained chickpeas thoroughly with a clean dish towel or paper towels and set aside.
2. Using a mortar and pestle or the flat side of a chef's knife, crack the coriander and cumin. Put the spices in a small bowl along with the flaky sea salt and red pepper flakes and set aside. In another small bowl, make the yogurt sauce. Whisk together yogurt, the minced garlic clove and a pinch of Kosher salt and set aside for serving.
3. In a large skillet, heat 2 tablespoons of olive oil over medium high heat. Add the chickpeas and a pinch of salt and cook, stirring occasionally, until crisped, 6 to 8 minutes. Stir in half of the spice mixture (save the rest for serving) and cook for another minute or two, until the spices are fragrant and toasted. Immediately transfer chickpeas to a paper towel-lined plate.

4. Season the beaten eggs with a pinch of salt and some black pepper. Heat the remaining 2 tablespoons oil over medium high and add the scallions and the 2 thinly sliced garlic cloves. Cook until golden at the edges, 1 to 2 minutes. Stir in the greens and a pinch of salt, and cook until wilted, 1 to 2 minutes. Carefully pour in the eggs and cook, stirring frequently, until just set, 1 minute.
5. To serve, spoon the scrambled eggs onto a dish, drizzle with garlic yogurt and top with chickpeas, cilantro, and more of the spice mixture. Squeeze a lime wedge on top and serve immediately.

Nutritional Value (Amount per Serving):

Calories: 632; Fat: 41.2; Carb: 37.03; Protein: 30.85

Mediterranean Inspired Avocado Toast with Pistachio Dukkah

Prep Time: 15 Minutes   Cook Time: 10 Minutes   Serves: 2

Ingredients:

- istachio Dukkah
- 1/2 cup raw pistachios
- 1/4 cup black or white sesame seeds
- 2 tablespoons cumin seeds or 2 teaspoons ground cumin
- 1 tablespoon coriander seeds or 1 teaspoon ground coriander
- 2 teaspoons dried oregano
- salt + pepper to taste
- vocado Toast
- 2 pieces crusty whole grain bread
- 2 tablespoons sun-dried tomatoes packed in oil reserve 1-2 tablespoon of the oil
- 2 tablespoons kalamata olives roughly chopped
- 1 ripe avocado pitted + sliced
- salt + pepper to taste
- juice + zest from 1/2 lemon
- 1-2 poached or fried eggs
- feta cheese crumbled
- large handful of micro greens + fresh herbs for topping

Directions:

Pistachio Dukkah

1. Heat a large skillet over medium heat. Add the pistachios and cook, stirring often until toasted, about 3-4 minutes. Remove the pistachios and add the sesame seeds, cumin, seeds and coriander seeds. Cook for 1-2 minutes or until toasted. Watch closely these can burn quickly. Remove from the skillet and toss with the pistachios. Allow to cool slightly.
2. Add all the toasted nuts and seeds + the oregano and a pinch of salt + pepper to a blender or food processor (or even a coffee grinder). Pulse until the pistachios are finely chopped. Do not over grind the mixture or you will end up with powder. Taste and add additional salt if needed. The dukkah

can be stored in an air tight container at room temp for up to 1 month.

Avocado Toast

1. Preheat the broiler to high. Rub you pieces of toast with the reserved olive oil in the sun-dried tomato jar and sprinkle lightly with salt. Place on a baking sheet and put under the broiler. Broil 30 seconds - 1 minute, watching closely as the toast can burn FAST. Once toasted, remove from the oven and top with sliced sun-dried tomatoes, olives and slices of avocado. Drizzle the avocado with lemon and then sprinkle with the dukkah and a little salt if needed. Add your eggs and sprinkle with salt, pepper and crushed red pepper flakes for heat (if desired) . Add some feta and micro greens. EAT...possibly with more dukkah as you go! :)

Nutritional Value (Amount per Serving):

Calories: 1055; Fat: 83.18; Carb: 53; Protein: 38.09

Socca (Farinata)

Prep Time: 10 Minutes   Cook Time: 20 Minutes   Serves: 4

Ingredients:

- 1 cup chickpea flour
- 1 cup water
- 1 tablespoon olive oil
- ½ teaspoon ground cumin
- salt and ground black pepper to taste
- 1 tablespoon vegetable oil for frying

Directions:

1. Combine chickpea flour, water, and olive oil in a bowl. Season with cumin, salt, and pepper to taste. Stir everything together until smooth. Set aside and let rest at room temperature for 2 hours.
2. Preheat the oven to 450 degrees F. Place a cast iron skillet in the oven until hot, 5 to 7 minutes.
3. Carefully remove skillet from oven, grease with oil and pour half of the the batter into the skillet, tilting so batter is evenly distributed.
4. Bake in the preheated oven until socca is set, about 7 minutes. Turn on broiler and brown for 1 minute. Remove from oven and slide onto a plate. Repeat with remaining batter.

Nutritional Value (Amount per Serving):

Calories: 154; Fat: 8.4; Carb: 14.48; Protein: 5.42

Chapter 2: Salads and Sides Dishes

Watermelon Salad With Herbed Yogurt Sauce

Prep Time: 30 Minutes   Cook Time: 0 Minute   Serves: 6

Ingredients:

- atermelon Salad
- 3 pounds ripe seedless watermelon (about 1/2 small round watermelon or 4 cups cubed), cut into 3/4" cubes
- 2 mini cucumbers or 1 small cucumber, thinly sliced into rounds
- 1/2 cup thinly sliced shallot (1 medium-to-large shallot)
- 3 tablespoons sherry vinegar or red wine vinegar
- 1/4 teaspoon fine sea salt
- 2 tablespoons extra-virgin olive oil
- Small handful fresh mint and basil leaves, torn if large, for garnish
- Flaky sea salt or kosher salt, to taste
- Freshly ground black pepper, to taste
- erbed Yogurt Sauce
- 1 cup Greek yogurt
- 1/3 cup lightly packed combination of fresh basil and fresh mint leaves
- 1 tablespoon extra-virgin olive oil
- 1 teaspoon honey or maple syrup
- Pinch of fine sea salt

Directions:

1. In a small bowl, combine the sliced shallot with the vinegar and 1/4 teaspoon salt. Toss to combine, and place in the refrigerator to lightly pickle while you prepare the rest of the salad.
2. Make the yogurt sauce: In a food processor, combine the yogurt, fresh herbs, olive oil, honey, and a pinch of salt. Blend until the herbs are broken into tiny pieces and the sauce is pale green. (If you don't have a food processor, finely chop the herbs and whisk the ingredients together in a bowl.)
3. Swirl the yogurt sauce (all of it) over the base of a large serving platter. Scatter the cubed watermelon on top, followed by the cucumber. Arrange the pickled shallot on top, and spoon the leftover vinegar over the salad.
4. Drizzle 2 tablespoons olive oil on top, sprinkle generously with fresh herbs, and season with salt and pepper, to taste. If you won't be serving immediately, place the salad in the refrigerator to stay chilled. This salad is best served within an hour or two.

Nutritional Value (Amount per Serving):

Calories: 302; Fat: 15.56; Carb: 24.94; Protein: 16.72

Fresh Herbed Avocado Salad

Prep Time: 25 Minutes   Cook Time: 5 Minutes   Serves: 4 To 6

Ingredients:

- erb-Pepita Mix
- 1/2 cup raw pepitas (green pumpkin seeds)
- 1/4 teaspoon chili powder
- 1/4 teaspoon extra-virgin olive oil
- Pinch of salt
- 1/2 cup chopped radish (about 3 medium)
- 1/2 cup chopped green onion
- 1/2 cup chopped fresh cilantro, parsley, basil, dill or any combination thereof
- 1 medium jalapeño, seeds and membranes removed, chopped (omit if sensitive to spice)
- verything Else
- 4 large just-ripe avocados
- 1/4 cup lime juice (about 1 to 2 limes)
- 2 tablespoons extra-virgin olive oil
- 2 teaspoons honey or maple syrup
- 1/2 teaspoon fine sea salt, plus flaky sea salt for finishing (optional)
- Lime zest for garnish, optional

Directions:

1. Since avocados start browning once they're cut, we're going to prepare everything else first. Toast the pepitas in a large skillet over medium heat, stirring often (don't let them burn!), until they're starting to turn golden on the edges and make little popping noises, about 3 to 5 minutes. Remove the skillet from the heat and stir in the chili powder, olive oil and pinch of salt. Set aside to cool.
2. Meanwhile, combine the chopped radish, green onion, herbs and jalapeño in a bowl, and set aside.
3. To prepare the dressing, whisk together the lime juice, olive oil, honey and salt in a small bowl. Set aside.
4. You can slice or dice the avocados however you'd like, but for the prettiest slices (like mine), first cut the avocados in half and remove the pits. Then cut the halves in half again to make long quarters. Peel the avocado skin off each quarter and carefully slice it into long strips.
5. To assemble, place the avocado in a medium serving bowl or platter. Drizzle the dressing all over them. Stir the toasted pepitas into the herb mix, then spoon it over the avocados. Finish the salad with optional flaky salt and/or lime zest.

Nutritional Value (Amount per Serving):

Calories: 367; Fat: 29.75; Carb: 25.36; Protein: 6.51

Spinach Salad With Apples, Walnuts, And Feta

Prep Time: 5-9 Minutes   Cook Time: 0 Minute   Serves: 4 To 6

Ingredients:
- 3 tablespoons olive oil
- 2 tablespoons apple cider vinegar
- 1 teaspoon Dijon mustard
- 1/2 teaspoon honey
- 1/4 teaspoon kosher salt
- 1/8 teaspoon freshly ground black pepper
- 1 (5-ounce) bag baby spinach (about 5 packed cups)
- 1 large tart apple, such as Granny Smith or Honeycrisp, cored and thinly sliced (about 1 1/2 cups)
- 4 ounces feta cheese, crumbled (about 1 cup)
- 1/2 cup walnuts, toasted and coarsely chopped

Directions:

1. Whisk together the olive oil, vinegar, mustard, honey, salt, and pepper in a large bowl.
2. Add the spinach and toss gently to coat in the vinaigrette. Add the apple, feta, and walnuts and toss gently again to combine. Serve immediately.

Nutritional Value (Amount per Serving):

Calories: 242; Fat: 20.08; Carb: 9.23; Protein: 7.51

Orzo with Spinach and Pine Nuts

Prep Time: 10 Minutes   Cook Time: 25 Minutes   Serves: 12

Ingredients:
- 1 package (16 ounces) orzo pasta
- 1 cup pine nuts
- 1 garlic clove, minced
- 1/2 teaspoon dried basil
- 1/2 teaspoon crushed red pepper flakes
- 1/4 cup olive oil
- 1 tablespoon butter
- 2 packages (6 ounces each) fresh baby spinach
- 1 teaspoon salt
- 1/4 teaspoon pepper
- 1/4 cup balsamic vinegar
- 2 cups crumbled feta cheese
- 1 large tomato, finely chopped

Directions:

1. In a large saucepan, cook pasta according to package directions.
2. Meanwhile, in a Dutch oven over medium heat, cook the pine nuts, garlic, basil and pepper flakes in oil and butter just until nuts are lightly browned.
3. Add the spinach, salt and pepper; cook and stir just until spinach is wilted, 4-5 minutes longer. Transfer to a large bowl.

4. Drain pasta. Stir into spinach mixture. Drizzle with vinegar; sprinkle with cheese and tomato.

Nutritional Value (Amount per Serving):

Calories: 224; Fat: 18.78; Carb: 9.16; Protein: 6.97

Tomato and Hearts of Palm Salad

Prep Time: 10 Minutes   Cook Time: 0 Minute   Serves: 8

Ingredients:

- 3 cups cherry tomatoes , sliced in half
- 1 15- ounce can hearts of palm , drained and sliced into ¼ inch rings
- ¼ cup red onion , thinly sliced or shaved
- ¼ cup Italian parsley , chopped
- ¼ cup vegetable oil
- 1 ½ tablespoon red vinegar
- 1 teaspoon sugar
- 1 teaspoon kosher salt
- ½ teaspoon freshly ground black pepper

Directions:

1. Combine tomatoes, hearts of palm, red onion and parsley in a large bowl. In a small bowl, mix the vegetable oil, vinegar, sugar and salt and pepper until sugar is dissolved. Pour vinaigrette over tomato mixture and gently mix. Add more salt and pepper to taste. Serve at room temperature.

Nutritional Value (Amount per Serving):

Calories: 160; Fat: 11.46; Carb: 9.07; Protein: 6.12

Whole Wheat Orzo Salad

Prep Time: 30 Minutes   Cook Time: 0 Minute   Serves: 8

Ingredients:

- 2-1/2 cups uncooked whole wheat orzo pasta (about 1 pound)
- 1 can (15 ounces) cannellini beans, rinsed and drained
- 3 medium tomatoes, finely chopped
- 1 English cucumber, finely chopped
- 2 cups crumbled feta cheese
- 1-1/4 cups pitted Greek olives (about 6 ounces), chopped
- 1 medium sweet yellow pepper, finely chopped
- 1 medium green pepper, finely chopped
- 1 cup fresh mint leaves, chopped
- 1/2 medium red onion, finely chopped

- 1/4 cup lemon juice
- 2 tablespoons olive oil
- 1 tablespoon grated lemon zest
- 3 garlic cloves, minced
- 1/2 teaspoon pepper

Directions:

1. Cook orzo according to package directions. Drain orzo; rinse with cold water.
2. Meanwhile, in a large bowl, combine remaining ingredients. Stir in orzo. Refrigerate until serving.

Nutritional Value (Amount per Serving):

Calories: 221; Fat: 14.45; Carb: 15.63; Protein: 9.19

Creamy Broccoli Slaw Salad

Prep Time: 35 Minutes   Cook Time: 0 Minute   Serves: 6-8

Ingredients:

- 3 cups broccoli florets (about 2 small heads), chopped into small pieces
- 1/2 cup purple cabbage, thinly sliced or shredded
- 1/3 cup feta cheese, crumbled
- 1/4 cup raisins
- 1/4 cup pine nuts, toasted
- 2 scallions, thinly sliced
- ressing:
- 1/3 cup mayonnaise (or sour cream or Greek yogurt)
- 1 tablespoon dijon mustard
- 1 tablespoon white wine vinegar
- 1 tablespoon lemon juice, freshly squeezed (about ½ lemon)
- 1 small shallot, finely chopped
- 1 teaspoon salt
- 1/4 teaspoon ground black pepper
- 1/4 cup extra virgin olive oil

Directions:

1. Cut the bottoms off the heads of broccoli so you're left with small sized florets. Then, trim the bottoms so they're not longer than 1-inch, and roughly chop.
2. In a large mixing bowl or serving bowl, combine broccoli, cabbage, feta, raisins, pine nuts, and scallions.
3. In a small mixing bowl, add mayonnaise, dijon mustard, white wine vinegar, lemon juice, shallot, salt, and pepper. Stir to combine. Slowly drizzle in olive oil and whisk until all ingredients are incorporated. You can add additional 1-2 tablespoons of olive oil if you prefer a thinner dressing.
4. Add dressing to the slaw, and toss all ingredients together. Let the slaw sit for 30 minutes, or up to overnight in the refrigerator. Serve cold or at room temperature.

Nutritional Value (Amount per Serving):

Calories: 154; Fat: 14.19; Carb: 2.47; Protein: 5.06

Grilled Halloumi Cheese

Prep Time: 5 Minutes   Cook Time: 5 Minutes   Serves: 12

Ingredients:

- 8 ounces chunk halloumi cheese cut into 1/3 to 1/2-inch slices
- 2 1/2 tablespoons extra virgin olive oil divided, plus additional for the grill
- 1/2 teaspoon dried oregano
- 1 lemon halved
- 1 1/2 teaspoons fresh thyme minced
- Pita bread optional, for serving

Directions:

1. Heat a grill to medium-high (about 400 degrees F). Make sure your grill is VERY clean or the halloumi may stick.
2. In a small bowl, stir together 1 1/2 tablespoon of olive oil and oregano.
3. Slice the Halloumi cheese into 1/3- to 1/2-inch slices.
4. Brush the marinade over both sides of the halloumi.
5. Generously oil the grill. Grill the halloumi for 2 to 6 minutes, turning once or twice, until grill marks appear. When lightly pressed the halloumi should give but not be runny (halloumi is a firm, not melty cheese). Place the lemon on the grill with the cut-sides down and let cook until grill marks appear. (To grill the pita, brush it with olive oil, then cook a minute or two on each side, until hot.)
6. Transfer the grilled halloumi and lemon to a platter. Drizzle the cheese with the remaining 1/2 tablespoon of olive oil. Squeeze the grilled lemon over the top. Sprinkle with thyme. Serve warm with pita, mixed into a salad, or however you please.

Nutritional Value (Amount per Serving):

Calories: 45; Fat: 3.72; Carb: 2.61; Protein: 0.45

Greek Chicken Marinade: A Delicious Way To Flavor Your Chicken

Prep Time: 35 Minutes   Cook Time: 10 Minutes   Serves: 2

Ingredients:

- 1 pound chicken breasts/ skinless boneless thighs
- 1 cup Greek yogurt
- 2 tablespoons olive oil
- 3 garlic cloves
- 1 lemon (organic, since we are

going to use the zest)
- 1 teaspoon dried thyme
- 1 teaspoon dried oregano

- ½ teaspoon dried rosemary
- 1 teaspoon dried parsley
- 1 teaspoon salt

Directions:

1. In a bowl combine the chicken breasts (you can cut them in strips like I did or in cutlets), the Greek yogurt, the olive oil, the dried herbs, and the salt.
2. Zest 2 teaspoons worth of the lemon zest directly into the bowl with the chicken.
3. Mix everything well, cover, and let marinate for at least 30 minutes before cooking.
4. Once the chicken has marinated heat 1 teaspoon olive oil in the pan and add the chicken to it once it gets hot.
5. Cook for 5-7 minutes and flip through the cooking.
6. Serve with a good Greek salad on the side for the perfect Mediterranean-themed lunch or dinner.

Nutritional Value (Amount per Serving):

Calories: 480; Fat: 23.55; Carb: 9.38; Protein: 55.74

Arugula Beet Salad

Prep Time: 10-15 Minutes   Cook Time: 0 Minute   Serves: 4 To 6

Ingredients:

- 3 tablespoons olive oil
- 2 tablespoons sherry vinegar
- 1 teaspoon Dijon mustard
- Kosher salt
- Freshly ground black pepper
- 1 (8-ounce) package steamed

beets, chopped
- 5 ounces arugula (about 5 packed cups)
- 4 ounces goat cheese, crumbled (about 1 cup)

Directions:

1. Whisk the olive oil, vinegar, mustard, a pinch of salt, and a few grinds of black pepper together in a large bowl. Add the beets and arugula and toss to combine. Add the goat cheese, toss again lightly, and serve.

Nutritional Value (Amount per Serving):

Calories: 317; Fat: 24.53; Carb: 3.53; Protein: 20.18

Easy Fresh Grilled Corn Salad

Prep Time: 10 Minutes   Cook Time: 5 Minutes   Serves: 6

Ingredients:

- 4 ears of corn, grilled (see my quick tutorial for how to grill corn)
- ½ English cucumber, chopped
- 2 carrots, chopped
- 1 to 2 shallots, or ½ small red onion, chopped
- 2 garlic cloves, minced
- 1 tablespoon fresh grated ginger root,
- ½ cup chopped fresh dill
- ½ cup chopped fresh cilantro or parsley
- Kosher salt
- 1 teaspoon cumin
- 2 tablespoons red wine vinegar
- 2 to 3 tablespoons extra virgin olive oil

Directions:

1. Follow this recipe to grill your corn over the gas stove or an outdoor grill (this will take 5 to 10 minutes). Allow the corn to cool before removing the kernels off the cob.
2. Invert a small bowl in the middle of a large mixing bowl. Hold an ear of corn upright, resting the tip of the cob over the small bowl in the center of your mixing bowl. Holding the cob steady with your non-dominant hand, use a sharp knife (you should be holding the knife with your dominant hand) and shave the kernels off the cob in long downward strokes.
3. Add the cucumber, carrots, shallots or red onions, minced garlic.
4. Add the herbs, and season with a good dash of kosher salt, cumin, and the grated ginger root.
5. Dress the salad with your red wine vinegar and a good drizzle of extra virgin olive oil. Toss until well-combined.

Nutritional Value (Amount per Serving):

Calories: 86; Fat: 2.94; Carb: 14.78; Protein: 2.38

Lemon Kale Salad

Prep Time: 5 Minutes   Cook Time: 0 Minute   Serves: 4

Ingredients:

- 5 cups kale, shredded
- 1 cup cherry tomatoes, halved
- 1/2 cup croutons
- 1/4 cup cheddar cheese, shredded
- or The Lemon Dressing:
- 2 tablespoons olive oil
- 2 tablespoons lemon juice, freshly squeezed
- 1 tablespoon Parmesan cheese, freshly grated
- 1/2 teaspoon garlic powder
- 1/4 teaspoon salt (or to taste)
- 1/4 teaspoon ground black pepper (or to taste)

Directions:

1. Place kale into a large mixing bowl or serving plate. Add cherry tomatoes, croutons, cheddar cheese.
2. In a small mixing bowl, stir to combine olive oil, lemon juice, Parmesan cheese, garlic powder, salt and pepper.
3. Pour the dressing over the salad and toss to combine.

Nutritional Value (Amount per Serving):

Calories: 120; Fat: 7.77; Carb: 12.03; Protein: 2.46

Cauliflower Casserole

Prep Time: 15 Minutes   Cook Time: 35 Minutes   Serves: 8

Ingredients:

- 2 medium heads of cauliflower cut into bite-size florets (about 3–4 pounds cauliflower, prior to being cut, or 5–6 cups florets)
- 2 tablespoons extra-virgin olive oil
- 1 teaspoon garlic powder
- 3/4 teaspoon kosher salt
- 1/2 teaspoon ground black pepper
- 1/4 teaspoon ground nutmeg
- 6 slices bacon
- 4 ounces reduced-fat cream cheese at room temperature
- 1/4 cup nonfat plain Greek yogurt
- 2/3 cup freshly grated Gruyere or similar melty, nutty, alpine-style cheese, divided
- 1/4 cup finely grated Parmesan cheese divided
- 3 tablespoons fresh chives chopped

Directions:

1. Place racks in the upper and lower thirds of your oven and preheat to 425 degrees F. Lightly coat a wide 3-quart (9x13) casserole dish, with nonstick spray, and line a rimmed baking sheet with parchment paper.
2. In a large bowl, toss the cauliflower florets with olive oil, garlic powder, salt, pepper, and nutmeg.
3. Transfer the cauliflower to the prepared casserole dish and spread it into an even layer. Keep the bowl handy. Roast cauliflower on the lower rack for 30 minutes, until the florets are tender and begin to brown.
4. Meanwhile, arrange the bacon strips in a single layer on the prepared foil-lined baking sheet. Bake on the upper rack until crisp, about 10 to 15 minutes.
5. Remove the bacon and cauliflower from the oven. Stir the cauliflower, spread it back into an even layer, and place it on the upper rack to continue cooking until the end of its baking time.

6. Transfer the bacon to a paper-towel-lined plate and lightly pat dry. Once cool enough to handle, roughly chop or crumble the bacon into small pieces.
7. In the same bowl that you used to toss the cauliflower, beat together the cream cheese and Greek yogurt until combined. Stir in 1/3 cup Gruyere cheese, 2 tablespoons of Parmesan cheese, and half of the chopped bacon.
8. Remove the roasted cauliflower from the oven and dollop the cream cheese mixture over the top. Sprinkle with the remaining 1/3 cup of Gruyere and 2 tablespoons of Parmesan.
9. Return the pan to the upper third of the oven and bake until the cheese is melted and gooey, about 5 to 7 minutes. Turn the oven to broil. Broil the casserole until golden on top, 1 to 3 minutes. Do not walk away, and watch carefully to make sure the cheese does not burn.
10. Remove from the oven and sprinkle with fresh chives and remaining bacon. Serve hot.

Nutritional Value (Amount per Serving):

Calories: 197; Fat: 16.32; Carb: 2.06; Protein: 10.65

Mediterranean Tuna Salad

Prep Time: 10 Minutes   Cook Time: 0 Minute   Serves: 2

Ingredients:

- 1 red bell pepper, finely diced
- 1 small shallot, minced
- 1 cup chopped English cucumber (or standard cucumber, peeled)
- 2 5-ounce cans white meat tuna
- 3 tablespoons capers, drained
- 2 tablespoon white wine vinegar
- 1 tablespoon olive oil
- 1 tablespoon Dijon mustard
- ¼ teaspoon kosher salt
- 2 tablespoons feta cheese crumbles (optional)

Directions:

1. Prep the red pepper, shallot and English cucumber as noted above.
2. Drain the tuna and place it in a medium bowl: mash it lightly with a fork. Add the chopped vegetables, capers, white wine vinegar, olive oil, Dijon mustard, feta (if using) and kosher salt and stir to combine. Taste and add more salt if desired. Stores up to 3 days refrigerated.

Nutritional Value (Amount per Serving):

Calories: 750; Fat: 50.69; Carb: 11.37; Protein: 60.42

Chapter 3: Grain, Pasta and Rice

Tomato-Garlic Lentil Bowls

Prep Time: 10 Minutes   Cook Time: 30 Minutes   Serves: 6

Ingredients:

- 1 tablespoon olive oil
- 2 medium onions, chopped
- 4 garlic cloves, minced
- 2 cups dried brown lentils, rinsed
- 1 teaspoon salt
- 1/2 teaspoon ground ginger
- 1/2 teaspoon paprika
- 1/4 teaspoon pepper
- 3 cups water
- 1/4 cup lemon juice
- 3 tablespoons tomato paste
- 3/4 cup fat-free plain Greek yogurt
- Optional: Chopped tomatoes and minced fresh cilantro

Directions:

1. In a large saucepan, heat oil over medium-high heat; saute onions 2 minutes. Add garlic; cook 1 minute. Stir in lentils, seasonings and water; bring to a boil. Reduce heat; simmer, covered, until lentils are tender, 25-30 minutes.
2. Stir in lemon juice and tomato paste; heat through. Serve with yogurt and, if desired, tomatoes and cilantro.

Nutritional Value (Amount per Serving):

Calories: 98; Fat: 3.05; Carb: 15.12; Protein: 5.11

Greek Cucumber Noodle Bowls With Turkey Meatballs

Prep Time: 10 Minutes   Cook Time: 0 Minutes   Serves: 1

Ingredients:

- 1/2 English Cucumber, spiralized
- 3-4 [Greek turkey meatballs]
- 1/4 cup chickpeas (drained and rinsed)
- 1 tablespoon crumbled reduced-fat feta cheese
- 1 tablespoon sliced kalamata olives
- thinly sliced red onion (as little or lot as you want!)
- 4-5 grape tomatoes, halved
- 2 tablespoons Sabra Classic Tzatziki Dip

Directions:

1. In a bowl, pile cucumber noodles. On top, add meatballs, chickpeas, feta, olives, onion, and tomatoes.
2. Top with Sabra Classic Tzatziki Dip and enjoy immediately.

Nutritional Value (Amount per Serving):

Calories: 863; Fat: 69.71; Carb: 21.52; Protein: 37.01

Zucchini Noodles With Arrabiata Chickpea Sauce

Prep Time: 15 Minutes   Cook Time: 15 Minutes   Serves: 2-3

Ingredients:

- rrabiata Sauce
- 1 small onion, chopped
- 2 cloves garlic, finely chopped
- 2 teaspoons extra virgin olive oil
- 1/2 tsp dried red pepper flakes
- 1 red bell pepper, chopped
- 3 or 4 diced tomatoes, seeded, with juice
- 2 tablespoons chopped fresh basil
- 1 can chickpeas, rinsed and drained
- ucchini Pasta
- 2 to 3 zucchinis
- olive oil
- sea salt
- black pepper

Directions:

1. Preheat the oven to 400 degrees Fahrenheit. In a medium saucepan, heat the oil over medium heat. Add the onions and garlic and sauté until the onion starts to caramelize, which will take about 10 minutes. Add the pepper flakes and red pepper and cook until the pepper softens, about 2 minutes.
2. Add the tomatoes and heat until the sauce begins to simmer. Lower heat and cook (uncovered) until thickened, about 15 minutes. Stir frequently.
3. Slice the ends off two to three zucchinis. Use a vegetable peeler to shave off strips of zucchini. It's easier than you think it'll be.
4. On a baking sheet, layer the zucchini a few layers deep, and drizzle with olive oil. Sprinkle some freshly ground black pepper on top.
5. Bake for about 10 minutes, until the zucchini has lost its crunch.
6. Back to the sauce: stir in the basil and chickpeas. Add salt and pepper, to taste. Cook about 5 more minutes, until everything is heated through. Serve generous portions of zucchini pasta topped with arrabiata sauce!

Nutritional Value (Amount per Serving):

Calories: 353; Fat: 10.25; Carb: 52.49; Protein: 16.2

Fusilli With Tahini-Yogurt Sauce And Nigella Seeds

Prep Time: 10 Minutes   Cook Time: 10 Minutes   Serves: 4-6

Ingredients:

- Fine sea salt
- 12 ounces whole grain fusilli, rotelle, or other pasta shells (gluten-free if desired)
- 2 tablespoons sesame seeds
- 1 teaspoon whole cumin seeds
- 1 teaspoon nigella seeds, optional
- 1 or 2 fresh hot red chiles, depending on your preference, seeds and veins removed for less heat
- 4 cloves garlic, peeled
- 1 cup plain Greek yogurt (whole milk or 2%, do not use nonfat)
- 1 cup low-fat sour cream
- 1/4 cup plus 2 tablespoons tahini
- 1/4 cup freshly squeezed lemon juice (1 to 2 lemons)
- 1/2 teaspoon fine sea salt
- 1/4 cup chopped fresh flat-leaf parsley, for garnish

Directions:

1. Bring a large pot of water to a rolling boil. Add salt as you see fit and then the pasta, stirring a few times. Return to a boil with the lid on; uncover and cook at a gentle boil until the pasta is al dente, according to the package directions.
2. While the water is coming to a boil, add the sesame, cumin, and nigella seeds to a medium skillet over medium heat. Toast, stirring frequently, until the seeds turn fragrant and the sesame turns golden, 3 to 5 minutes. Immediately scrape the seeds onto a plate.
3. Cut half of the chile into fine rings and set aside. Add the remaining chile and the garlic to the bowl of a food processor, fitted with the metal blade. Process until minced, scraping down the sides as needed. Add the yogurt and sour cream and blend until creamy. Add the tahini, lemon juice, and salt and process until smooth.
4. While the pasta is cooking, transfer the sauce to a 12-inch skillet. Gently heat over medium-low, stirring occasionally, until warmed through, about 5 minutes (do not bring to a boil, as the yogurt will curdle).
5. To finish, dip a heatproof measuring cup into the pasta pot to reserve 3/4 cup cooking liquid. Drain the pasta and add it to the skillet with the sauce. Add about half of the reserved liquid. Toss vigorously to combine for 1 to 2 minutes, adding a bit more cooking liquid as needed, until you have a creamy sauce. Sprinkle with the seed mixture, the chile rings, and the parsley. Serve at once.

Nutritional Value (Amount per Serving):

Calories: 414; Fat: 14.19; Carb: 61.87; Protein: 12.66

Lemon Dill Chicken Pasta With Goat Cheese

Prep Time: 20 Minutes   Cook Time: 10 Minutes   Serves: 4

Ingredients:

- 8 ounces whole wheat bowtie pasta or pasta of your choice
- 1 tablespoon extra virgin olive oil plus 3 teaspoons, divided, plus additional for tossing pasta
- 10 ounces boneless skinless chicken breasts (about 1 large or 2 small breasts)
- 1/2 medium red onion thinly sliced
- 1/2 teaspoon kosher salt
- 1/4 teaspoon black pepper
- 1 cup green peas fresh or frozen
- Zest of 1 lemon
- 3 tablespoons freshly squeezed lemon juice about 1 lemon
- 1 1/2 cups fresh chopped spinach
- 2 tablespoons chopped fresh dill
- 4 ounces goat cheese

Directions:

1. Bring a large pot of salted water to a boil and cook pasta until al dente, according to package directions. Reserve 1 cup of the pasta water, then drain. Toss the drained pasta with a bit of olive oil to prevent sticking, then set aside.
2. Heat 1 tablespoon olive oil in a large skillet over medium-high. Once hot, add the chicken and sauté until cooked through, 4 to 6 minutes (be careful as the oil may splatter). With a slotted spoon, remove to plate lined with paper towels and set aside.
3. Reduce pan heat to medium. Add 1 teaspoon olive oil to the skillet, the onions, salt, and pepper, and cook until fragrant and beginning to soften; about 1 minute. Add the peas and cook until heated through (about 1 minute for fresh or 3 minutes for frozen).
4. Add the reserved chicken, reserved pasta, remaining 2 teaspoons olive oil, lemon zest, and lemon juice. If the pasta seems to dry, add a little of the reserved pasta water.
5. Just before serving, stir in the spinach, dill, and goat cheese. Serve warm.

Nutritional Value (Amount per Serving):

Calories: 364; Fat: 16.04; Carb: 25.88; Protein: 31.56

Zucchini Pasta with Roasted Red Pepper Sauce and Chicken

Prep Time: 1 Hours   Cook Time: 30 Minutes   Serves: 4

Ingredients:

- 6 roma tomatoes
- 3 red bell peppers, chopped
- 1 large sweet onion, halved
- 3 tablespoons extra-virgin olive oil
- 4 cloves garlic
- 1 (28 ounce) can crushed tomatoes
- 1 cup tightly packed fresh basil leaves, chopped
- salt and ground black pepper to taste

- 2 yellow summer squash, cut into spirals using a spiral slicer
- 2 zucchini, cut into spirals using a spiral slicer
- 2 cooked chicken breast halves, cubed
- 1 tablespoon grated Parmesan cheese, or to taste

Directions:

1. Preheat grill for medium heat and lightly oil the grate.
2. Grill tomatoes, bell peppers, and onion halves on the preheated grill until well charred, about 15 minutes. When peppers are cool enough to handle, split with a knife and remove seeds.
3. Heat olive oil in a large skillet; cook and stir garlic until fragrant, about 1 minute. Stir canned crushed tomatoes, basil, grilled tomatoes, bell peppers, and onion into skillet; bring to a boil, reduce heat, and simmer until vegetables are tender, about 10 minutes. Puree vegetable mixture with a stick blender; season with salt and pepper and keep at a simmer.
4. Bring a large pot of water to a boil; drop in summer squash and zucchini spirals and cook until tender, about 3 minutes. Drain water from pot; lay spirals on paper towels to drain completely.
5. Place squash spirals on individual plates; top with a portion of cooked chicken, a generous amount of red pepper sauce, and Parmesan cheese.

Nutritional Value (Amount per Serving):

Calories: 172; Fat: 6.98; Carb: 24.74; Protein: 7.17

Mediterranean-Style Toasted Orzo Pasta With Parmesan And Sundried Tomatoes

Prep Time: 5 Minutes   Cook Time: 10 Minutes   Serves: 4

Ingredients:

- extra virgin olive oil (Our Italian Nocellara EVOO is a good choice here)
- 1 ½ cups orzo pasta
- Kosher salt
- 5 cloves garlic (minced)
- red pepper flakes (optional)
- ½ lemon (juice of)
- 1 cup parsley (chopped, packed)
- ½ cup dill (chopped)
- ⅓ cup sundried tomatoes in olive oil (chopped)
- black pepper
- ½ to ¾ cup grated parmesan (more to your liking)

Directions:

1. In a large saucepan, eat 2 tablespoons extra virgin olive oil over medium-high. Add the orzo and cook, tossing around, until toasted to a beautiful golden brown.
2. Add at least 7 cups of boiling water to the saucepan and season well with

kosher salt. Cook the pasta in boiling water to al dante according to the package instructions (about 7 to 8 minutes).

3. Just before the pasta is fully cooked (about 5 minutes), take a cup of the starchy pasta water and save it aside for now.

4. In a large pan, warm ½ cup extra virgin olive oil over medium heat. Add the garlic and season with a pinch of kosher salt and red pepper flakes, if using. Cook, tossing regularly, until just fragrant. Add the lemon juice and ½ cup of the pasta cooking water. Raise the heat if needed to bring to a boil. Add the parsley and dill.

5. When the pasta is ready, drain and add it to the pan and toss to combine. Season with kosher salt and black pepper. Add the sundried tomatoes and a bit of the grated parmesan. Toss to combine. If needed, add a little more of the pasta cooking water. Finish with more Parmesan and red pepper flakes, if you like.

Nutritional Value (Amount per Serving):

Calories: 207; Fat: 10.31; Carb: 23.43; Protein: 6.6

Spicy Sausage Pasta

Prep Time: 10 Minutes   Cook Time: 35 Minutes   Serves: 4-6

Ingredients:

- 3 Tbsp extra virgin olive oil
- 1 red bell pepper, diced
- 6oz mushrooms, diced
- 6 garlic cloves, finely chopped
- 20oz spicy Italian sausage, casings removed
- 28oz canned crushed tomatoes
- 1/2 - 1 tsp red chili flakes (optional)
- 1/2 cup red wine
- 1.5 tsp dried oregano
- 1.5 tsp dried basil
- 1.5 tsp sugar or to taste
- salt to taste
- 8oz rigatoni, or pasta of your choice
- 2 Tbsp fresh basil, for garnish
- Parmesan cheese, for garnish

Directions:

1. Heat extra virgin olive oil over medium high heat, and sauté bell pepper and mushrooms for 8-10 minutes.

2. Push the vegetables to the edges, and add sausage in the middle of the pan. Cook the sausage while breaking it into chunks.

3. Once the sausage starts browning up a bit, mix it in well with the peppers and mushrooms.

4. Add in garlic and red chili flakes, and continue cooking till the meat is brown all over.

5. Add in crushed tomatoes along with dried oregano, dried basil, salt and

sugar. Cook for 5 minutes.

6. Add in wine and simmer for 20 minutes.

7. Meanwhile, cook the pasta according to package directions. Once pasta is cooked, drain and add the pasta to the sauce. Stir gently to combine. Taste and adjust the sauce for salt, sugar or chili flakes according to taste.

8. Garnish it with fresh basil strips and parmesan cheese shavings.

Nutritional Value (Amount per Serving):

Calories: 598; Fat: 46.99; Carb: 17.39; Protein: 27.66

Make-Ahead Mediterranean Egg Casserole

Prep Time: 10 Minutes   Cook Time: 35-40 Minutes   Serves: 8 To 10

Ingredients:

- 1 teaspoon olive oil, plus more for the pan
- 1/2 small red onion
- 2 cloves garlic
- 1 (14-ounce) can water-packed artichokes
- 1 cup grape or cherry tomatoes (about 5 ounces)
- 1 tablespoon fresh oregano leaves
- 4 ounces feta cheese, crumbled (about 1 cup)
- 1/2 ounce Parmesan cheese, finely grated (about 1/4 cup)
- 1 1/4 teaspoons kosher salt, divided
- 6 ounces baby spinach (about 6 cups)
- 12 Eggland's Best large eggs
- 2 cups whole or 2% milk
- 1/4 teaspoon freshly ground black pepper

Directions:

1. Arrange a rack in the middle of the oven and heat the oven to 375°F. Coat a 9x13-inch baking dish with olive oil.

2. Prepare the vegetables and cheeses: Thinly slice 1/2 small red onion. Finely chop 2 garlic cloves. Drain and coarsely chop 1 can artichokes. Halve 1 cup grape or cherry tomatoes, or quarter if large. Finely chop 1 tablespoon fresh oregano leaves. Crumble 4 ounces 1 cup feta cheese (about 1 cup). Finely grate 1/2 ounces Parmesan cheese (about 1/4 cup).

3. Heat 1 teaspoon olive oil in a large skillet over medium-high heat until shimmering. Add the red onion and 1/2 teaspoon of the kosher salt, and cook until soft, 2 to 3 minutes. Add the garlic and artichokes and cook until the garlic is fragrant, about 1 minute. Add 6 ounces spinach (about 6 cups) and cook until just wilted, about 2 minutes.

4. Transfer the vegetables to the prepared baking dish and arrange in an even layer. Sprinkle the tomatoes and feta cheese evenly over the vegetables.

5. Whisk the Parmesan, oregano, 12 Eggland's Best large eggs, 2 cups whole or 2% milk, 1/4 teaspoon black pepper, and remaining 3/4 teaspoon kosher salt together in a large bowl until combined. Pour the egg mixture over the vegetables.
6. Bake until puffed, set, and an instant-read thermometer inserted into the center reads 160°F, about 30 minutes. Let the casserole cool for 10 minutes before serving.

Nutritional Value (Amount per Serving):

Calories: 208; Fat: 13.22; Carb: 11.93; Protein: 10.91

Eggplant Pasta

Prep Time: 10 Minutes   Cook Time: 20 Minutes   Serves: 4

Ingredients:

- 12 ounces whole wheat pasta or gluten free pasta if needed, any shape you like (I used fusilli)
- 2 tablespoons extra virgin olive oil
- 1 medium eggplant cut into 1/2-inch cubes (about 1 pound)
- 1 large red bell pepper cut into 1/4 x 1-inch strips
- 2 cloves garlic minced
- 1/2 teaspoon kosher salt
- 1/2 teaspoon black pepper
- 1/4 teaspoon crushed red pepper flakes
- 12 ounces prepared tomato pasta sauce
- 1/2 cup kalamata olives
- Zest and juice of 1 medium lemon
- 1/4 cup chopped fresh herbs such as parsley or basil
- Freshly grated Parmesan cheese for serving

Directions:

1. Bring a large pot of salted water to a rolling boil. Add the pasta and cook until al dente, according to package directions. Drain, toss with a bit of olive oil to prevent sticking, and set aside.
2. Meanwhile, heat oil in a large nonstick skillet over medium. Add the chopped eggplant and bell pepper and cook until just softened, about 5 minutes, stirring occasionally.
3. Add the garlic and sauté just until fragrant, about 30 seconds. Add the salt, black pepper, and red pepper flakes and stir to combine.
4. Stir in the tomato sauce, then the olives. Let simmer 5 minutes, or until heated through. Stir in the lemon juice and zest.
5. Stir the pasta into the eggplant tomato sauce, adding a little more of the prepared pasta sauce as needed to moisten the noodles. Served topped with chopped fresh herbs and Parmesan. Enjoy immediately.

Nutritional Value (Amount per Serving):

Calories: 365; Fat: 6.84; Carb: 60.84; Protein: 16.64

Moroccan Freekeh Pilaf Recipe

Prep Time: 10 Minutes   Cook Time: 25 Minutes   Serves: 4

Ingredients:

- 1 teaspoons ground cumin
- 1/2 teaspoon turmeric
- 1/2 teaspoon ground ginger
- 1/4 teaspoon ground cloves
- 1/8 teaspoon ground cayenne pepper
- 1/2 teaspoon ground cardamom
- 1/2 teaspoon ground cinnamon
- 1/4 teaspoon ground coriander
- 1/4 teaspoon ground allspice
- 1 tablespoon olive oil
- 1/2 cup golden raisins
- 1/2 cup diced dried apricots
- 1 teaspoon kosher salt
- grated zest of one orange (about 1 teaspoon)
- 2 cups chicken broth
- 1/2 cup orange juice (fresh squeezed is best)
- 1 cup uncooked cracked freekeh
- 3 tablespoons chopped fresh mint

Directions:

1. Heat a large saucepan over medium heat. Stir in the cumin, turmeric, ginger, cloves, cayenne, cardamom, coriander, and allspice; toast until fragrant, stirring, about 2 to 3 minutes. Stir in oil, raisins, apricots, salt, orange zest, chicken broth, orange juice. Bring to a boil.
2. Once boiling, stir in the freekeh and reduce to simmer (medium-low). Cover and cook for 20 minutes or until liquid is absorbed. Keep covered and remove from heat – let stand 5 minutes.
3. Fluff with a fork, and fold in chopped mint. Serve warm or cold.

Nutritional Value (Amount per Serving):

Calories: 681; Fat: 25.81; Carb: 53.47; Protein: 60.3

Summer Coconut Chickpea Curry with Rice and Fried Halloumi

Prep Time: 15 Minutes   Cook Time: 25 Minutes   Serves: 4

Ingredients:

- 1/4 cup + 4 tablespoons extra virgin olive oil
- 1 can (14 ounce) chickpeas, drained
- kosher salt and black pepper
- 2 zucchini, or summer squash, diced
- 2 ears sweet corn, kernels

removed from the cob
- 1 shallot, chopped
- 1 inch fresh ginger, grated
- 2 cloves garlic, minced or grated
- 1 1/2 tablespoons yellow curry powder
- 1/2 teaspoon cayenne pepper, more or less to taste
- 1 can (14 ounce) coconut milk
- 2 tablespoons tahini (sesame seed paste)
- juice and zest from 1/2 a lemon
- 1/4 cup fresh cilantro, roughly chopped (basil can be used)
- 8 ounces Halloumi cheese, sliced into 1/4 inch pieces (omit if vegan)
- 2 cups cooked basmati rice
- sesame seeds, green onions, and Persian cucumbers, for serving (optional)

Directions:

1. Heat 1/4 cup olive oil in a large pot over medium heat. When the oil shimmers, add the chickpeas and season with salt and pepper. Cook, stirring occasionally until the chickpeas begin to crisp, about 5 minutes. Carefully remove 1/2 cup of chickpeas and reserve for topping, only if desired.
2. To the remaining chickpeas, add the zucchini, corn, shallot, garlic, and ginger. Season with salt and pepper. Cook the veggies another 5-10 minutes or until they just begin to soften.
3. Stir in the curry powder and cayenne and cook until fragrant, about 1 minute. Add the coconut milk, 1/3-1/2 cup water, and the tahini. Stir to combine, bring the mixture to a simmer over medium heat, cook 5-10 minutes or until the sauce thickens slightly. If the sauce thickens too much, add additional water to thin. Remove from the heat and stir in the lemon juice and zest, and cilantro.
4. Meanwhile, cook the halloumi. Heat 2 tablespoons olive oil in a large skillet over medium heat. When the oil shimmers, add the halloumi and cook until golden, about 3 minutes per side. Remove from skillet.
5. To serve, divide the rice among bowls and spoon the curry overtop. Top with halloumi, the reserved chickpeas, and cucumbers. Enjoy!

Nutritional Value (Amount per Serving):

Calories: 867; Fat: 55.31; Carb: 85.64; Protein: 34.6

Chapter 4: Fish and Seafood

Shellfish Cioppino Recipe

Prep Time: 15 Minutes   Cook Time: 40 Minutes   Serves: 6

Ingredients:

- ¼ cup extra virgin olive oil
- 1 medium yellow onion (chopped)
- 2 medium red bell peppers (seeded and chopped)
- 5 cloves garlic (chopped)
- 1 teaspoon finely ground real salt
- 2 bay leaves
- 1 teaspoon dried oregano
- 1 teaspoon dried thyme
- ½ teaspoon crushed red pepper flakes
- 1 cup white wine
- 4 cups fish stock
- 48 oz diced tomatoes
- 1 teaspoon worcestershire sauce
- 1 ½ pounds crab legs
- 1 ½ pounds shrimp (deveined)
- 1 ½ pounds clams
- chopped flat-leaf parsley (to serve)
- lemon (to serve)

Directions:

1. In a large heavy bottom pot heat butter and olive oil over medium high heat. Add onions, leeks, celery, bay leaves, and a pinch of sea salt. Let vegetables soften and become translucent, about 7 minutes. But careful to not let them brown, lower heat as necessary. Add red and green bell peppers and let cook down for an additional 4 minutes. Lower heat to medium and add garlic and dried spices. Stir frequently and allow spices to become very fragrant and sauté for about 3 minutes.
2. Deglaze with white wine and add seafood broth, clam juice, strained tomatoes, chopped tomatoes, tomato paste, and fish sauce. Bring to a boil, then lower heat to lowest setting. Taste and add salt as needed. If you are starting with a homemade seafood broth, then you will probably need to add more salt; a flat taste is a good indicator. Allow sauce to cook uncovered for 20 minutes. Stir intermittently, careful to avoid scorching or sticking.
3. Add crab legs and let simmer while covered for 5 minutes. Then add shrimp and clams and cook covered until the clams open. Lastly, add scallops and cook until firm, about 3 more minutes. Sprinkle with chopped parsley and serve immediately with lemon wedges and starch of choice (sourdough is mighty good, but a side of potatoes or rice works). Don't forget plenty of napkins!

Nutritional Value (Amount per Serving):

Calories: 516; Fat: 20.21; Carb: 28.76; Protein: 53.41

Sheet-Pan Honey Tahini Salmon with Chickpeas and Couscous

Prep Time: 5 Minutes   Cook Time: 20 Minutes   Serves: 6

Ingredients:

- ¼ cup honey
- ¼ cup tahini
- 3 tablespoons fresh lemon juice, plus 1 lemon, halved
- 2 tablespoons extra-virgin olive oil
- Pinch of kosher salt and freshly ground black pepper
- 2 pounds salmon fillets
- One 15-ounce can chickpeas, rinsed and drained
- 1 cup couscous
- ¼ cup chopped fresh parsley, plus more for garnish
- ¼ cup golden raisins, plus more for garnish
- ⅛ teaspoon crushed red pepper flakes
- 1¼ cups vegetable or chicken stock (store-bought or homemade)
- ⅓ cup toasted chopped almonds
- 1 tablespoon za'atar
- Labne or Greek yogurt, for serving

Directions:

1. Preheat the oven to 400°F.
2. In a small bowl, whisk together the honey, tahini, lemon juice, olive oil, salt and pepper. Using a pastry brush or spoon, evenly coat the salmon fillets with the sauce on all sides. Place the fillets in the center of a sheet pan along with the halved lemon, cut side up, and roast for 10 minutes.
3. After 10 minutes, carefully slide the sheet pan out of the oven and add the chickpeas, couscous, chopped parsley, raisins, pepper flakes in an even layer surrounding the salmon and lemon. Pour the stock over the couscous mixture, and return to the oven. Cook until the salmon is medium-rare and flakes easily with a fork and the couscous is cooked through and tender, 6 to 8 minutes.
4. To serve, garnish with more parsley and raisins and the za'atar and almonds. Serve with labne or Greek yogurt on the side.

Nutritional Value (Amount per Serving):

Calories: 714; Fat: 32.32; Carb: 48.63; Protein: 58.22

Lemon Salmon With Garlic And Thyme

Prep Time: 5 Min   Cook Time: 5 Min   Serves: 4

Ingredients:

- Four 5- to 6-ounce salmon fillets
- Extra virgin olive oil, as needed
- Kosher salt and freshly ground black pepper
- 1 whole lemon, zested and sliced
  into thin rounds
- ½ teaspoon dried thyme
- 4 to 5 five garlic cloves, peeled and lightly crushed

Directions:

1. Preheat the oven to 400°F.
2. Place the salmon fillets in a baking dish, and drizzle lightly with olive oil. Season with salt and pepper, then sprinkle evenly with the lemon zest and thyme. Arrange the lemon slices on top of the fillets, and add the garlic cloves to the dish.
3. Transfer to the oven and bake until the salmon is cooked through and flakes with a fork, 18-20 minutes (adjust the baking time if your fillets are very thick or thin).

Nutritional Value (Amount per Serving):

Calories: 280; Fat: 19.07; Carb: 1.84; Protein: 24.01

Pesto Salmon With Burst Tomatoes

Prep Time: 7-10 Minutes   Cook Time: 7-11 Minutes   Serves: 4

Ingredients:

- 1 pound cherry or grape tomatoes (about 3 cups)
- 1 medium shallot
- 4 (6-ounce) skin-on salmon fillets
- 1 1/2 teaspoons kosher salt, divided
- 1/2 teaspoon freshly ground black pepper, divided
- 4 tablespoons olive oil, divided
- 1/4 cup basil pesto, store-bought or homemade, divided

Directions:

1. Halve 1 pound cherry or grape tomatoes. Dice 1 medium shallot. Pat 4 salmon fillets dry with paper towels, then season on both sides with 1 teaspoon of the kosher salt and 1/4 teaspoon of the black pepper.
2. Heat 2 tablespoons of the olive oil in a large nonstick skillet with a lid over medium-high heat until shimmering. Add the salmon skin-side up and sear until golden-brown on the bottom, about 4 minutes.
3. Transfer the salmon skin-side down to a plate (it will not be cooked through). Add the remaining 2 tablespoons olive oil to the pan. Add the tomatoes and shallot, season with the remaining 1/2 teaspoon kosher salt and 1/4 teaspoon black pepper, and cook, stirring occasionally, until the tomatoes begin to blister and burst, 1 to 2 minutes.
4. Reduce the heat to medium and return the salmon skin-side down to the

pan, nestling it into the tomatoes. Spread 1/4 cup basil pesto onto the salmon with the back of a spoon. Cover and cook the salmon to desired doneness, 2 to 5 minutes depending on the thickness of the fillets. An instant-read thermometer inserted into the middle of the thickest fillet should register 120°F to 130°F for medium-rare or 135°F to 145°F if you prefer it more well-done.

Nutritional Value (Amount per Serving):

Calories: 699; Fat: 36.36; Carb: 18.62; Protein: 76.4

Grill Juicy, Flavorful Shrimp

Prep Time: 15 Minutes   Cook Time: 4 Minutes   Serves: 6

Ingredients:

- 1 cup plain full-fat yogurt
- 2 tablespoons freshly squeezed lemon juice
- 2 cloves garlic, minced
- 5 large fresh mint leaves, finely chopped
- 1 1/2 pounds large (20 to 25 per pound) uncooked shrimp, thawed if frozen and peeled and deveined

Directions:

1. Soak the skewers: If using wooden skewers, soak in water while preparing the shrimp.
2. Make the marinade: Combine the yogurt, lemon juice, garlic, and mint in a large bowl.
3. Marinade the shrimp: Add the shrimp to the yogurt mixture and toss to coat. Cover and refrigerate for 30 minutes. Meanwhile, prepare the grill.
4. Prepare the grill for direct heat: Heat half of the burners of a gas grill to high or prepare a chimney's worth of lump charcoal for a charcoal grill. Make sure that the grill grates are clean and debris-free. Preheat the gas grill for at least 10 minutes.
5. Skewer the shrimp: Thread the shrimp onto the skewers, leaving any yogurt that clings to the shrimp. Skewer through the thickest part of each shrimp, arranging 6 to 8 shrimp per skewer. Place on a large plate or baking sheet.
6. Grill the shrimp: Grill the shrimp over direct heat for about 2 minutes per side, flipping as soon as the first side begins to turn pink along the edges. Cook until the shrimp are opaque and slightly charred.

Nutritional Value (Amount per Serving):

Calories: 120; Fat: 2.04; Carb: 6.04; Protein: 19.3

Mediterranean Baked White Fish

Prep Time: 10 Minutes   Cook Time: 15 Minutes   Serves: 6

Ingredients:

- 1 ½ lb white fish fillet such as cod or halibut, (1 to 1 ½ in thickness)
- Kosher salt and ground black pepper
- Extra virgin olive oil
- Juice of ½ lemon more for later
- 8 ounces cherry tomatoes, halved
- 3 ounces pitted olives, halved (I used a combination of kalamata olives and green olives)
- 3 tablespoons minced red onion
- 4 to 5 garlic cloves, minced
- 1 tablespoon fresh thyme leaves
- 2 teaspoons dried oregano

Directions:

1. Heat the oven to 425 degrees F.
2. Pat the fish dry and season with salt and pepper on both sides. Brush a 9 ½ x 13-inch baking dish with a little extra virgin olive oil and put the fish in it. Squeeze ½ lemon juice all over the top of the fish.
3. In a medium mixing bowl, combine the tomatoes, olives, onions, garlic and spices. Add a very small pinch of salt and ground pepper. Add a generous drizzle (about 3 tablespoons extra virgin olive oil) toss to combine.
4. Pour the tomato and olive mixture over the fish.
5. Bake in the heated oven for 15 to 20 minutes (this will depend on the thickness of your fish).
6. Remove from the heat and serve.

Nutritional Value (Amount per Serving):

Calories: 142; Fat: 3.49; Carb: 29.56; Protein: 1.77

Sweet-Chili Salmon with Blackberries

Prep Time: 10 Minutes   Cook Time: 15 Minutes   Serves: 4

Ingredients:

- 1 cup fresh or frozen blackberries, thawed
- 1 cup finely chopped English cucumber
- 1 green onion, finely chopped
- 2 tablespoons sweet chili sauce, divided
- 4 salmon fillets (6 ounces each)
- 1/2 teaspoon salt
- 1/2 teaspoon pepper

Directions:

1. In a small bowl, combine blackberries, cucumber, green onion and 1

tablespoon chili sauce; toss to coat. Sprinkle salmon with salt and pepper.

2. Place fillets on greased grill rack, skin side down. Grill, covered, over medium-high heat or broil 4 in. from heat 10-12 minutes or until fish flakes easily with a fork, brushing with remaining chili sauce during the last 2-3 minutes of cooking. Serve with blackberry mixture.

Nutritional Value (Amount per Serving):

Calories: 716; Fat: 30.16; Carb: 18.66; Protein: 87.54

Salmon Chowder Recipe

Prep Time: 5 Minutes   Cook Time: 25 Minutes   Serves: 1

Ingredients:

- 2 tablespoons salted butter
- 2 medium leeks (white and light-green parts only, sliced thin)
- 1 bulb fennel (cored and sliced thin)
- 1 teaspoon finely ground real salt
- ½ cup white wine
- 30 ounces fish stock
- 1 pound red potatoes (quartered)
- 1 ½ pounds wild-caught salmon fillets (skin removed and chopped into pieces)
- ½ cup heavy cream
- 2 tablespoons chopped fresh dill

Directions:

1. Warm the butter in the bottom of a Dutch oven set over medium-low heat. When the butter releases its foam, toss in the sliced leek and fennel. Sprinkle the aromatics with salt, and let them sweat, covered and stirring occasionally, until soft and tender - about 8 minutes.

2. Uncover the pot, pour in the wine and fish stock, and then add the potatoes. Turn up the heat to medium-high and simmer until the potatoes are tender, about 20 minutes. Drop the salmon into the pot, cover, and allow it to continue simmering until the fish is opaque and cooked through, about 3 to 5 minutes. Remove from the heat, stir in the cream and dill. Salt the chowder as it suits you, and then ladle into soup bowls.

Nutritional Value (Amount per Serving):

Calories: 808; Fat: 22.64; Carb: 101.51; Protein: 52.34

Pesto-Crusted Grouper

Prep Time: 5 Minutes   Cook Time: 10 Minutes   Serves: 2

Ingredients:

- 1 (9 ounce) grouper fillet
- salt and ground black pepper to taste
- 2 tablespoons panko bread crumbs
- ¼ tablespoon Greek seasoning (such as Cavender's)
- 2 teaspoons pesto
- 2 tablespoons butter

Directions:

1. Season grouper fillet with salt and pepper. Mix bread crumbs and Greek seasoning in a small bowl. Rub pesto over the grouper and top with bread crumbs.
2. Melt butter in a skillet over medium heat. Place fillet in the skillet and cook for 3 to 4 minutes. Carefully turn over and cook until fillet is cooked through, 3 to 4 minutes. Turn over once more, being careful to leave the panko breading in place. Split fillet in half for 2 serves.

Nutritional Value (Amount per Serving):

Calories: 343; Fat: 22.04; Carb: 7.85; Protein: 28.14

Zippy Shrimp Skewers

Prep Time: 10 Minutes   Cook Time: 5 Minutes   Serves: 6

Ingredients:

- 2 tablespoons brown sugar
- 2 teaspoons cider vinegar
- 1-1/2 teaspoons canola oil
- 1 teaspoon chili powder
- 1/2 teaspoon salt
- 1/2 teaspoon paprika
- 1/4 teaspoon hot pepper sauce
- 3/4 pound uncooked medium shrimp, peeled and deveined

Directions:

1. In a large shallow dish, combine the first 7 ingredients; add shrimp. Turn to coat; cover and refrigerate for 2-4 hours.
2. Drain and discard marinade. Thread shrimp onto 6 metal or soaked wooden skewers. Grill, uncovered, on a lightly oiled rack over medium heat or broil 4 in. from the heat until shrimp turn pink, 2-3 minutes on each side.

Nutritional Value (Amount per Serving):

Calories: 59; Fat: 1.23; Carb: 3.7; Protein: 7.84

Sheet Pan Pistachio-Crusted Cod With Fall Vegetables

Prep Time: 10 Minutes   Cook Time: 35-40 Minutes   Serves: 4

Ingredients:

- 1 medium red onion
- 1 pound Brussels sprouts
- 1 pound sweet potatoes (about 2 medium)
- 3 tablespoons plus 1 teaspoon olive oil, divided
- 1 teaspoon kosher salt, plus more for seasoning
- 1/2 teaspoon freshly ground black pepper
- 3/4 cup shelled, roasted, and salted pistachios
- 1 clove garlic
- 4 (3/4-inch-thick) skinless cod fillets (6 to 8 ounces each)
- 2 tablespoons Dijon mustard

Directions:

1. Arrange a rack in the middle of the oven and heat the oven to 425°F.
2. Prepare the following, placing them on a rimmed baking sheet as you complete them: Trim and halve 1 pound Brussels sprouts. Cut 1 pound sweet potatoes (no need to peel) into 1-inch chunks. Cut 1 medium red onion into 1-inch chunks.
3. Drizzle with 3 tablespoons of the olive oil, season with 1 teaspoon kosher salt and 1/2 teaspoon black pepper, and toss to combine. Spread out in an even layer. Roast for 25 minutes. Meanwhile, coat the fish with the pistachios.
4. Place 3/4 cup shelled, roasted, and salted pistachios, 1 garlic clove, and the remaining of 1 teaspoon olive oil in the bowl of a food processor fitted with the blade attachment. Pulse until coarsely chopped, about 40 pulses. Transfer to a wide, shallow bowl or pie plate.
5. Pat 4 skinless cod fillets dry with a paper towel. Lightly season all over with kosher salt and black pepper. Brush 2 tablespoons Dijon mustard on the tops of the fish. Place the fish mustard-side down in the chopped pistachios and press firmly to coat so that they adhere. Place the fish pistachio-side up on a large plate. If there are any pistachios left, use your hands to press them into any open spaces on the fish. Refrigerate until the vegetables are ready.
6. Remove the baking sheet from the oven. Reduce the oven temperature to 400°F. Toss the vegetables, then push them aside to create 4 open spaces for the fish. Use a spatula to carefully transfer the fish to the open spaces. Roast until the fish is opaque and flakes easily, and the vegetables are tender, 10 to 15 minutes more.

Nutritional Value (Amount per Serving):

Calories: 479; Fat: 21.83; Carb: 45.3; Protein: 30.57

Parchment Baked Lemon Salmon and Potatoes with Dill Yogurt

Prep Time: 10 Minutes   Cook Time: 20 Minutes   Serves: 4

Ingredients:

- 1/4 cup extra virgin olive oil
- 2 cloves garlic, minced or grated
- 2 lemons
- 1 tablespoon chopped fresh dill
- 2 teaspoons smoked paprika
- 2 small potatoes, very thinly sliced using a mandolin
- 4 6-8 ounce salmon fillets, skinned
- kosher salt and pepper
- fresh arugula and basil, for serving
- 1 cup plain greek yogurt
- ill Yogurt
- 1 tablespoon chopped fresh dill
- juice of 1 lemon
- 1 pinch crushed red pepper flakes

Directions:

1. Preheat the oven to 400 degrees F. Fold 4 large pieces of parchment paper (about 15x16 inches) in half. Open, and lay on half flat.
2. In a small bowl, stir together the olive oil, garlic, juice of 1 lemon, dill, smoked paprika and a pinch of salt and pepper.
3. Working on one side of the creased parchment, layer the potatoes, and season with salt and pepper. Place the salmon over the potatoes and drizzle with the olive oil sauce, and top with 2 lemons slices. Repeat with the remaining ingredients to make 4 packets.
4. To close, fold the parchment over salmon, pinching to seal the open sides and create a half-moon-shaped packet. Place on a rimmed baking sheet. Transfer to the oven and bake until the potatoes are tender, about 18-20 minutes.
5. Meanwhile, in a medium bowl, stir together the yogurt, lemon juice, dill, and a pinch of crushed red pepper.
6. Serve the salmon topped with dill yogurt, arugula, and basil. Enjoy!

Nutritional Value (Amount per Serving):

Calories: 331; Fat: 11.81; Carb: 42.86; Protein: 16.07

Chapter 5: Pizza, Wraps, and Sandwiches

Greek-Inspired Burgers with Herb-Feta Sauce

Prep Time: 25 Minutes   Cook Time: 12 Minutes   Serves: 4

Ingredients:

- 1 cup nonfat plain Greek yogurt
- ¼ cup crumbled feta cheese
- 3 tablespoons chopped fresh oregano, divided
- ¼ teaspoon lemon zest
- 2 teaspoons lemon juice
- ¾ teaspoon salt, divided
- 1 small red onion
- 1 pound ground lamb or ground beef
- ½ teaspoon ground pepper
- 2 whole-wheat pitas, halved, split and warmed
- 1 cup sliced cucumber
- 1 plum tomato, sliced

Directions:

1. Preheat grill to medium-high or preheat broiler to high.
2. Mix yogurt, feta, 1 tablespoon oregano, lemon zest, lemon juice and 1/4 teaspoon salt in a small bowl.
3. Cut 1/4-inch-thick slices of onion to make 1/4 cup. Finely chop more onion to make 1/4 cup. (Reserve any remaining onion for another use.) Mix the chopped onion and meat in a large bowl with the remaining 2 tablespoons oregano and 1/2 teaspoon each salt and pepper. Form into 4 oval patties, about 4 inches by 3 inches.
4. Grill or broil the burgers, turning once, until an instant-read thermometer registers 160 degrees F, 4 to 6 minutes per side. Serve in pita halves, with the sauce, onion slices, cucumber and tomato.

Nutritional Value (Amount per Serving):

Calories: 372; Fat: 18.4; Carb: 15.62; Protein: 35.22

Cheesy Garlic Dinner Rolls

Prep Time: 1 Hour 15 Minutes   Cook Time: 20 Minutes   Serves: 10-12

Ingredients:

- or The Dough:
- 3 grams active dry yeast
- 180 grams milk (3/4 cup), at room temperature
- 50 grams butter, softened at room temperature (1/4 cup)
- 8 grams sugar (2 teaspoons)
- 6 grams salt (1 teaspoon)
- 1 egg
- 375 grams all purpose flour (3 cups)
- or The Cheese Filling:
- 1/2 (8 oz.) package cream cheese (1/2 cup), at room temperature

- 1/4 cup mozzarella cheese, shredded
- or The Garlic Topping:
- 2 tablespoons garlic, minced
- 1 tablespoon butter, melted
- 2 tablespoons mozzarella cheese, shredded
- 1 tablespoon Parmesan cheese, finely grated
- 2 tablespoons green onions, finely chopped
- 1 egg, beaten (for egg wash)
- 1 tablespoon white sesame seeds (optional, for garnish)

Directions:

Prepare The Dough:

1. In a large mixing bowl, combine yeast, milk, butter, sugar, salt and egg, and whisk until well combined and yeast is dissolved. The butter might still be a little lumpy in the mixture at this point.
2. Add flour and stir well to combine until no dry flour is visible in the bowl. Scrape down the sides of the bowl with a spatula, as needed.

Knead The Dough:

1. Transfer the dough mixture onto a clean and lightly greased surface. The oil will help keep the dough from sticking to your hands initially. You can even lightly oil your hands too.
2. Knead the dough for 5-10 minutes until the dough ball is smooth and not sticky at all. A well kneaded dough is smooth and can hold its shape. To test if the dough is well-kneaded, give the dough ball a firm poke with your finger. The indentation should bounce right back. If it doesn't bounce back and stays like a dimple, keep kneading for a few more minutes.

Shape And Stuff The Dinner Rolls:

1. In a small mixing bowl, add cream cheese and mozzarella. Stir with a spatula until well combined.
2. Roll the dough into a log and use a knife or bench scraper to divide it into 10-12 equal pieces (or 8-10 equal pieces with a larger piece in the middle).
3. Flatten the dough and add 1.5 tablespoons of the cheese mixture into the centre of the dough. Press all edges into the centre to seal so that the cheese doesn't escape out during baking. Turn it over and cup the dough in your palm, making circular motions. It should take less than 30 seconds to roll each piece into a smooth ball.

Proof The Dinner Rolls:

1. Arrange the cheese filled dough balls on a large skillet or parchment-lined baking sheet. Leave 1/2-inch of space in between each dough ball.
2. Cover the pan with plastic cling wrap to prevent the dough from drying out. When the dough loses moisture, it tends to form hard skin around its surface, which creates a crust when baking. Let the rolls rest and rise for 1 hour. The rolls should almost double in size. Note that placing the rolls in a warmer area will help them rise faster.

Bake The Dinner Rolls:

1. Preheat oven to 375 F.
2. In a small mixing bowl, stir to combine garlic, melted butter, shredded mozzarella, grated parmesan, and chopped green onions. Apply egg wash over each roll and add a spoonful of the garlic cheese mixture on top. The egg wash helps the toppings stick to the surface of the rolls. Sprinkle some sesame seeds on top (optional, for garnish).
3. Bake in the preheated oven for 20 minutes, or until the tops of the rolls are golden brown.
4. Let the rolls cool on a wire cooling rack for 15 minutes before serving.

Nutritional Value (Amount per Serving):

Calories: 264; Fat: 13.56; Carb: 27.17; Protein: 8.28

Mediterranean Roasted Red Pepper Pizza

Prep Time: 15 Minutes   Cook Time: 15 Minutes   Serves: 6

Ingredients:

- 1/2 pound pizza dough
- 2 tablespoons olive oil
- 2 garlic, minced or grated
- 1 teaspoon dried basil
- 1 teaspoon dried oregano
- 1/2 teaspoon crushed red pepper flakes
- kosher salt and pepper
- 1/2 cup pitted kalamata olives
- 1/3 cup oil packed sun-dried
- tomatoes, oil drained and sliced
- 1/4 cup marinated artichokes, drained
- 8 ounces mozzarella, torn or shredded
- 1/2 cup shredded fontina cheese
- 4-8 pepperoni slices (optional)
- 2 red bell peppers, very thinly sliced
- fresh basil, for topping

Directions:

1. Preheat oven to 425 degrees F. Grease a baking sheet with olive oil.
2. On a lightly floured surface, push/roll the dough out until it is very thin. For SUPER thin pizza, divide the dough into two and roll out. Transfer the dough to the prepared baking sheet. Spread the dough with olive oil. Add the garlic, basil, oregano, crushed red pepper flakes, and a pinch each of salt and pepper. Spread evenly over the dough. Add the olives, sun-dried tomatoes, artichokes, and cheese. Top with pepperoni and bell peppers. Transfer to the oven and bake 10-15 minutes or until the crust is crisp and the cheese has melted. Remove the pizza from the oven and top with basil. EAT!

Nutritional Value (Amount per Serving):

Calories: 299; Fat: 16.73; Carb: 17.78; Protein: 20.74

Chicken Caesar Wrap

Prep Time: 15 Minutes   Cook Time: 0 Minute   Serves: 4

Ingredients:

- 1/2 cup dry-packed sun-dried tomatoes or oil packed sun-dried tomatoes
- 1/3 cup homemade Caesar dressing or Caesar dressing of choice, divided
- 1 teaspoon Worcestershire sauce optional for a more intense flavor
- 2 1/2 cups cooked diced or shredded chicken breast about 2
- medium breasts; see notes
- 1 romaine lettuce heart chopped (about 4 cups)
- 1/3 cup shredded Parmesan cheese (no green can please!)
- 1/4 teaspoon kosher salt
- 1/4 teaspoon ground black pepper
- 4 whole wheat wraps or flatbreads such as pita, naan, or tortillas

Directions:

1. If using dry-packed sun-dried tomatoes, place them in a small bowl and cover with hot water to rehydrate. Let sit for a few minutes while you prepare the rest of the ingredients, then drain. If using oil-packed sun-dried tomatoes, simply pat them dry.
2. Place the Caesar dressing in a medium bowl. Stir together with 1 teaspoon Worcestershire sauce. Add the chicken, romaine, sun-dried tomatoes, Parmesan, salt, and black pepper. Toss to coat in the dressing.
3. For each chicken Caesar wrap, lay your wrap down on a work surface. Pile each wrap with 1/4 of the chicken Caesar filling. Roll snugly, tucking in two opposing sides to keep the filling from falling out. If desired, slice in half. Enjoy immediately or wrap in foil, parchment paper, or plastic wrap and refrigerate for up to 4 hours.

Nutritional Value (Amount per Serving):

Calories: 482; Fat: 8.98; Carb: 91.18; Protein: 16.48

Caprese Pizza Rolls With Prosciutto

Prep Time: 1 Hour 15 Minutes   Cook Time: 20-25 Minutes   Serves: 12

Ingredients:

- 1 pound fresh, refrigerated pizza dough
- 1/4 cup loosely packed fresh basil leaves
- 2 cloves garlic
- 1 pint cherry tomatoes (about 2 cups)
- 1/2 small lemon

- 1 tablespoon olive oil
- 1/4 teaspoon kosher salt
- Pinch red pepper flakes
- All-purpose flour, for dusting
- 3 ounces thinly sliced prosciutto (about 6 slices)
- 1 (8-ounce) ball fresh mozzarella cheese (not packed in water)

Directions:

1. If refrigerated, let 1 pound pizza dough sit out at room temperature for about an hour. Arrange a rack in the middle of the oven and heat the oven to 425°F. Line a rimmed baking sheet with parchment paper.
2. Coarsely chop 1/4 cup loosely packed fresh basil leaves. Mince 2 garlic cloves and place in a medium bowl. Quarter 1 pint cherry tomatoes and add to the bowl. Finely grate the zest of 1/2 small lemon into the bowl (reserve the zested lemon for another use). Add 1 tablespoon olive oil, 1/4 teaspoon kosher salt, and a pinch red pepper flakes to the bowl and toss to combine.
3. Dust a work surface lightly with all-purpose flour. Place the pizza dough on the flour and firmly pat it into a rough 6x8-inch rectangle. Using a floured rolling pin, roll out the dough as thin as possible, about 10 inches wide and 12 inches long, with a long side closer to you. If the dough starts to spring back as you roll, let it rest for a few minutes, then try again.
4. Arrange 3 ounces thinly sliced prosciutto evenly on the dough, leaving about a 1-inch border at the top and bottom. Use a slotted spoon to scatter the tomato mixture over the prosciutto, leaving any juices in the bowl behind. Sprinkle half of the basil leaves over the tomatoes. Firmly pat 8 ounces fresh mozzarella cheese all over with a paper towel to remove excess moisture, then tear into bite-sized pieces and scatter over the tomatoes.
5. Starting at the long end closest to you, roll up the dough tightly into a log. Pinch the seam in the dough closed. Cut the log crosswise with a serrated knife into 12 pieces. Use a pastry scraper or flat spatula to transfer the rolls cut-side up to the baking sheet, spacing them evenly apart. Tuck any toppings that may have fallen out back between the folds.
6. Bake until the cheese is bubbly and the rolls are light golden brown on top, 20 to 25 minutes. Let cool for 10 minutes on the baking sheet. Sprinkle with the remaining 2 tablespoons chopped fresh basil before serving.

Nutritional Value (Amount per Serving):

Calories: 216; Fat: 8.37; Carb: 28.38; Protein: 6.71

Avocado Caprese Chicken Wraps

Prep Time: 20 Minutes   Cook Time: 0 Minute   Serves: 4

Ingredients:

- 4 Flatout Flatbreads (I use Multi-grain with Flax)
- illing
- 1 1/4 cups shredded Rotisserie chicken
- 1/4 cup any combo of mayo, sour cream, or yogurt (I use 2T mayo, 2T sour cream)
- 2 cups chopped romaine lettuce
- 2 small Roma tomatoes, sliced
- 4 oz. sliced mozzarella cheese (may sub shredded)
- 1 large avocado or 2 small, sliced
- 1/2 cup basil, chiffonade
- 4 strips Cooked and crumbled bacon (optional)
- alsamic Chicken "Marinade"
- 3 tablespoons balsamic vinegar
- 1 tablespoon olive oil
- 1 1/2 teaspoons Dijon mustard
- 1 1/2 teaspoons lemon juice
- 1 teaspoon brown sugar
- 1/2 tsp EACH garlic pwdr, onion pwdr, salt
- 1/4 teaspoon pepper

Directions:

1. Whisk all the Balsamic Chicken Marinade ingredients together in a medium bowl. Remove 2 teaspoons and add to a bowl with your chopped tomatoes. Toss to coat.
2. To the remaining marinade, add chicken, stir until evenly coated.
3. Spread the entire surface of each Flatbread with 1 tablespoon mayo/sour cream/yogurt.
4. Evenly divide lettuce between flatbreads in a row in the bottom third of the flatbread. Top evenly with chicken, avocado, cheese, tomato, basil and bacon.
5. Roll up flatbreads and slice in half. Serve with extra balamic vinegar if desired.

Nutritional Value (Amount per Serving):

Calories: 946; Fat: 63.72; Carb: 23.34; Protein: 68.24

Grilled Cheese Roll Ups

Prep Time: 10 Minutes   Cook Time: 4 Minutes   Serves: 10

Ingredients:

- 10 slices cheddar cheese slices
- 10 slices white toast bread
- 2-3 tablespoons butter

Directions:

1. Remove the crust from the bread and use a rolling pin to roll it out to 1/4-inch thick.
2. Place a slice of cheddar cheese into the center of the bread and roll it up tightly.

3. Melt butter in a large skillet over medium heat and place grilled cheese roll ups on top and cook until all sides are crispy and golden brown, about 3-4 minutes. You may have to cook in 2 batches.
4. Transfer onto a plate lined with paper towel to absorb any excess butter. Serve warm.

Nutritional Value (Amount per Serving):

Calories: 208; Fat: 13.27; Carb: 13.11; Protein: 8.89

Spinach Feta Breakfast Wraps

Prep Time: 10 Minutes   Cook Time: 10 Minutes   Serves: 4

Ingredients:

- 10 large eggs
- 1/2 pound (about 5 cups) baby spinach
- 4 whole-wheat tortillas (about 9 inches in diameter, burrito-sized)
- 1/2 pint cherry or grape tomatoes, halved
- 4 ounces feta cheese, crumbled
- Butter or olive oil
- Salt
- Pepper

Directions:

1. In a large bowl, whisk the eggs until the whites and yolks are completely combined. Place a large skillet over medium heat and add enough butter or olive oil to coat the bottom. When the butter is melted or the oil is hot, pour in the eggs and stir occasionally until the eggs are cooked. Stir in a pinch of salt and a generous amount of black pepper, then transfer to a large plate to cool to room temperature.
2. Rinse or wipe down the skillet, place it back over medium heat, and add another pat of butter or oil. Add the spinach and cook, stirring often, until the spinach is just wilted. Spread the cooked spinach on another large plate to cool to room temperature.
3. Arrange a tortilla on a work surface. Add about a quarter each of the eggs, spinach, tomatoes, and feta down the middle of the tortilla and tightly wrap (see How To Wrap a Burrito). Repeat with the remaining three tortillas. Place the wraps in a gallon zip-top bag and freeze until ready to eat. If freezing for more than a week, wrap the burritos in aluminum foil to prevent freezer burn. To reheat, microwave on high for 2 minutes.

Nutritional Value (Amount per Serving):

Calories: 432; Fat: 21.5; Carb: 43.13; Protein: 20.1

Socca Pizza With Summer Squash And Feta

Prep Time: 1 Hour 5 Minutes   Cook Time: 20 Minutes   Serves: 2

Ingredients:

- occa Pizza Crust
- 1 cup (120 grams) chickpea flour
- 1 cup water
- 1/4 cup olive oil, divided
- 1 to 2 garlic cloves, pressed or minced
- 1/4 teaspoon sea salt
- izza Toppings
- 1/2 cup shredded mozzarella
- 1/4 cup crumbled feta
- 1 small zucchini and/or yellow squash (I used both but had leftovers of each), ribboned with a vegetable peeler and/or julienne peeler and tossed lightly in olive oil
- 5 pitted Kalamata olives, sliced in half lengthwise
- Small handful sun-dried tomatoes (either oil-packed or Trader Joe's dried kind)
- 1 small sprig fresh thyme, optional

Directions:

1. In a bowl, whisk together the chickpea flour, water, 2 tablespoons of the olive oil, garlic and salt. Let the mixture rest at room temperature for 1 hour.
2. Turn on the broiler with a rack positioned 8 inches from heat. Place a 10-inch ovenproof skillet (preferably cast iron) in the oven to preheat.
3. Once the skillet is hot, carefully remove it from the oven (it's crazy hot, wear oven mitts!). Pour in 1 tablespoon olive oil and swirl the pan around so the oil is evenly distributed. Pour in the chickpea batter and return the skillet to the broiler. Cook for 5 to 8 minutes, until the socca is set and the edges are browning and pulling away from the sides of the pan. Remove from oven, turn off broiler and turn oven to 425 degrees Fahrenheit.
4. Spread the remaining 1 tablespoon olive oil on top of the socca (it will soak right in). Top the socca with mozzarella, then distribute the ribboned/ julienned squash on top. Sprinkle olives and sun-dried tomatoes on top, then sprinkle feta over the pizza.
5. Return the skillet to the oven and bake for 8 to 10 minutes, until the cheese is browning and the socca is crisp. Remove from oven and sprinkle fresh thyme on top. Let the pizza cool for 2 to 3 minutes before slicing into 4 pieces and serving.

Nutritional Value (Amount per Serving):

Calories: 1232; Fat: 68.63; Carb: 107.11; Protein: 50.62

Italian Eggplant Sandwich

Prep Time: 15 Minutes   Cook Time: 20 Minutes   Serves: 4

Ingredients:

- 2 medium eggplants, about 1 pound each
- Extra virgin olive oil
- Kosher salt
- Black pepper
- 4 to 6 medium-sized ripe tomatoes (we used Village Farms Sinfully Sweet Campari)
- 1/2 pound fresh mozzarella cheese
- ¼ cup basil pesto (purchased, Best Basil Pesto, Cashew Pesto, Walnut Pesto, or Vegan Cashew Pesto)
- ¼ cup olive spread or tapenade (purchased or homemade Kalamata Olive Spread)
- 4 artisan hoagies or focaccia bread (or 8 pieces of bread, like Sourdough Bread or Dutch Oven Bread)
- Basil leaves, for the garnish (optional)

Directions:

1. Cut the eggplant into 1/2-inch thick rounds.
2. Grilled method: Preheat a grill to medium high heat (375 to 450 degrees Fahrenheit). Make sure the grates are clean. Right before grilling, brush each side with olive oil. Sprinkle the tops with kosher salt and fresh ground pepper. Grill for 10 to 20 minutes (depending on the grill), turning halfway through, until tender and grill marks form. Alternatively, you can use a grill pan on the stovetop: heat the pan and grill the eggplant slices until they are tender and grill marks form.
3. Roasted method: Or, you can roast the eggplant! Go to Perfect Roasted Eggplant and follow the instructions for eggplant rounds.
4. Toast the bread: Toast the bread in the remaining minutes on the grill, or place it in the oven for a few minutes to toast it.
5. Assemble the sandwiches: Thinly slice the tomatoes. Tear the mozzarella into pieces. Spread pesto on the cut side of one piece of bread, and olive spread on the cut side of the other bread. Place grilled eggplant on the bread, and top with mozzarella, sliced tomatoes, and basil, if using. Top with the other bread slice. If desired, wrap in aluminum foil to help contain the mess when eating!
6. Make ahead notes: The sandwiches can be made a few hours in advance for picnics. If doing so, you may want to slice the tomatoes and let them sit on a cutting board for several minutes to drain excess liquid.

Nutritional Value (Amount per Serving):

Calories: 329; Fat: 7.62; Carb: 42.19; Protein: 26.59

Grilled Mediterranean Vegetable Sandwich

Prep Time: 20 Minutes   Cook Time: 40 Minutes   Serves: 6

Ingredients:

- 1 eggplant, sliced into strips
- 2 red bell peppers
- 2 tablespoons olive oil, divided
- 2 portobello mushrooms, sliced
- 3 cloves garlic, crushed
- 4 tablespoons mayonnaise
- 1 (1 pound) loaf focaccia bread

Directions:

1. Preheat the oven to 400 degrees F.
2. Brush eggplant and red bell peppers with 1 tablespoon olive oil; use more if necessary, depending on sizes of vegetables. Place on a baking sheet and roast in the preheated oven. Roast eggplant until tender, about 25 minutes; roast peppers until blackened. Remove from oven and set aside to cool.
3. Meanwhile, heat 1 tablespoon olive oil and cook and stir mushrooms until tender. Stir crushed garlic into mayonnaise. Slice focaccia in half lengthwise. Spread mayonnaise mixture on one or both halves.
4. Peel cooled peppers, core, and slice. Layer eggplant, peppers, and mushrooms in focaccia.
5. Wrap sandwich in plastic wrap; place a cutting board on top of it and weight it down with some canned foods. Allow sandwich to sit for 2 hours before slicing and serving.

Nutritional Value (Amount per Serving):

Calories: 138; Fat: 8.86; Carb: 12.79; Protein: 4.04

Garlic Mushroom Focaccia Pizza

Prep Time: 3 Hour 10 Minutes   Cook Time: 25 Minutes   Serves: 12

Ingredients:

- izza Dough:
- 3 grams instant yeast or active dry yeast (1 teaspoon)
- 200 grams water (3/4 cup)
- 300 grams all-purpose flour (2 + 1/2 cups)
- 6 grams salt (1 teaspoon)
- 3 tablespoons olive oil, divided
- oppings:
- 1 cup fresh mozzarella, grated
- 1 cup sautéed garlic mushrooms, sliced
- 1/4 cup tomato sauce
- 1/4 cup fresh basil leaves (about 15 leaves)
- 1 tablespoon olive oil

Directions:

Prepare The Pizza Dough (First Rise):

1. In small cup, dissolve instant yeast in water and stir to mix together (the mixture should start to bubble and develop a yeasty aroma).
2. In a large mixing bowl, add flour and salt. Pour in yeast mixture and mix with a silicone spatula until fully combined, scraping down the sides of the bowl (there should be no dry flour particles visible).
3. Knead the dough for 5 minutes until it turns into a smooth dough ball. Add and spread one tablespoon oil over the dough ball to coat. This helps prevent the dough from drying out.
4. Cover the bowl with plastic cling wrap and let it sit at room temperature for 2 hours (or in the refrigerator overnight) until the dough at least doubles in size. The gluten in dough will completely loosen over a long period of fermentation, which makes the dough stretch out easily.

Shape The Pizza Dough (Second Rise):

1. Spread 2 tablespoons olive oil evenly on a quarter sheet baking pan. Transfer the dough into the sheet pan and gently spread it out to all corners. The oil not only makes the dough spread easily and prevents it from sticking to the pan but it also creates a brown crispy crust when baked.
2. Cover the sheet pan with plastic cling wrap and let the dough rise for 1 hour until the pizza dough almost rises to the rim of the sheet pan, about 1-inch thick. If the dough springs back from the edges, allow the gluten in dough relax for a few minutes and stretch it out.

Assemble And Bake:

1. Preheat the oven to 450 F.
2. When the dough is ready, evenly spread mozzarella cheese, garlic mushrooms, tomato sauce, basil and olive oil on top. Bake for 20 to 25 minutes or until the top turns golden brown.
3. Let the pizza cool for 5 minutes before slicing.

Nutritional Value (Amount per Serving):

Calories: 297; Fat: 9.19; Carb: 40.7; Protein: 12.67

Chapter 6: Poultry and Turkey

Greek Chicken And Potatoes Recipe

Prep Time: 15 Minutes   Cook Time: 1 Hour   Serves: 6

Ingredients:

- or Chicken And Potatoes
- 3 lb chicken pieces, bone in and skin on (I used 2 breasts and 3 legs)
- Salt
- 4 gold potatoes (about 2 lb), scrubbed clean, cut into thin wedges
- 1 medium yellow onion, halved then sliced
- 1 tsp black pepper
- 1 lemon, sliced
- 1 cup chicken broth
- 6 to 12 pitted quality kalamata olives, optional
- Fresh parsley, for garnish
- or The Lemon-Garlic Sauce (Can Also Be Used As Marinade)
- 1/4 cup extra virgin olive oil (I used Private Reserve Greek extra virgin olive oil)
- 1/4 cup lemon juice
- 12 fresh garlic cloves, minced
- 1 1/2 tbsp dried rosemary (or dried oregano)
- 1/2 tsp ground nutmeg
- ides (Optional)
- Greek Salad
- Tzatziki Sauce
- Pita Bread

Directions:

1. Preheat oven to 350 degrees F.
2. Pat chicken dry and season generously with salt (lift the skins and apply salt underneath as well).
3. Arrange potato wedges and onions in the bottom of a baking dish or pan. Season with salt and 1 tsp black pepper. Add the chicken pieces (see optional step in notes).
4. Make the lemon-garlic sauce. In a small mixing bowl, whisk together 1/4 cup extra virgin olive oil with lemon juice, minced garlic, rosemary, and nutmeg. Pour evenly over the chicken and potatoes.
5. Arrange lemon slices on top. Pour chicken broth into the pan from one side (do not pour broth over the chicken).
6. Bake in heated oven uncovered for 45 minutes to 1 hour, until chicken and potatoes are tender. (Chicken's internal temperature should register at 165 degrees F). If you like, place the pan under the broiler briefly to allow the chicken skins to gain more color (watch carefully).
7. Remove from heat and add kalamata olives, if you like. Garnish with a little bit of fresh parsley.
8. Serve with Greek salad Taztaziki sauce and a side of pita bread, if you like. Enjoy!

Nutritional Value (Amount per Serving):

Calories: 808; Fat: 36.71; Carb: 57.03; Protein: 61.78

Crispy Za'atar Chicken and Cauliflower

Prep Time: 10 Minutes   Cook Time: 45 Minutes   Serves: 4

Ingredients:

- 2 tablespoons (30ml) melted ghee or clarified butter
- 3 tablespoons (23g) za'atar
- 1 tablespoons (15ml) fresh lemon juice
- 1½ tsp (9g) kosher salt
- 1 head cauliflower, cut into florets (about 4 cups or 400g)
- 1 red onion, cut into 1-inch wedges
- 3 garlic heads, tops trimmed
- 2 lemons, halved
- 2 pounds (905g) bone-in, skin-on chicken thighs (about 4 large thighs)

Directions:

1. Preheat the oven to 425°F and line a rimmed baking sheet with foil.
2. In a small bowl, combine the melted ghee, za'atar, lemon juice and salt. Place the cauliflower, onion, garlic heads, halved lemons and chicken on the prepared baking sheet. Add the seasoning mixture and toss until evenly coated. Arrange everything into a single layer on the baking sheet.
3. Bake until the chicken is cooked, 40 to 45 minutes, then broil on high until the skin is crispy, about 1 minute. Squeeze the roasted garlic cloves out of the heads and sprinkle over the chicken, then serve.

Nutritional Value (Amount per Serving):

Calories: 2172; Fat: 212.73; Carb: 20.64; Protein: 47.21

Mediterranean Chicken Sheet Pan Dinner

Prep Time: 15 Minutes   Cook Time: 40 Minutes   Serves: 4

Ingredients:

- ¼ cup extra-virgin olive oil
- lemon, juiced
- 2 tablespoons balsamic vinegar
- 1 teaspoon dried tarragon
- 1 teaspoon dried oregano
- 1 teaspoon paprika
- 1 teaspoon salt
- ½ teaspoon black pepper
- 4 chicken thighs with skin
- 1 small red onion, sliced into petals
- 8 mini bell peppers, halved lengthwise and seeded
- 1 pound baby potatoes, halved
- 1 lemon, sliced
- ¼ cup crumbled feta cheese
- ¼ cup fresh parsley, chopped
- 8 pitted kalamata olives

Directions:

1. Preheat the oven to 425 degrees F. Line a large rimmed baking sheet with aluminum foil.
2. Whisk olive oil, juice of 1 lemon, vinegar, tarragon, oregano, paprika, salt, and pepper together in a large bowl.
3. Add chicken thighs, onion, baby bell peppers, and potatoes. Stir until everything is evenly coated.
4. Transfer vegetable-chicken mixture to the prepared baking sheet and spread in an even layer. Scatter lemon slices over the vegetables, making sure to leave the chicken uncovered so that the skin will brown.
5. Bake in preheated oven for about 40 minutes. Remove from oven and top with feta, parsley, and olives.

Nutritional Value (Amount per Serving):

Calories: 251; Fat: 10.13; Carb: 35.17; Protein: 7.84

Chicken Puttanesca

Prep Time: 5 Minutes   Cook Time: 40 Minutes   Serves: 6

Ingredients:

- 3 pounds bone-in, skin-on chicken pieces (I used 4 thighs and 4 drumsticks)
- Kosher salt
- Ground black pepper
- Extra virgin olive oil
- 1 teaspoon Italian seasoning
- 1 lemon, juiced
- ¼ cup extra virgin olive oil
- 4-8 anchovy filets
- 5 large garlic cloves, minced
- 1 (28-ounce) can whole peeled San Marzano tomatoes
- ½ cup pitted kalamata olives, sliced
- 3 tablespoons drained capers
- 2 teaspoons dried oregano
- 1 teaspoon red pepper flakes, optional
- ½ cup chopped parsley leaves, for garnish

Directions:

1. Season the chicken: Use paper towels to pat the chicken pieces dry. Season well with kosher salt and black pepper on both sides. Rub some salt and pepper underneath the skin as well.
2. Sear the chicken: In a large nonstick skillet set over medium-high heat, add 3 tablespoons of olive oil. Once the oil begins to shimmer, add the chicken, skin side down. Cook until the skin is crispy and golden brown, about 5-8 minutes. Flip and cook until the second side is golden brown as well, about 5 minutes more.

3. Season and rest the chicken: Transfer the chicken to a large tray and sprinkle with Italian seasoning. Pour the lemon juice over the chicken. Set it aside for now.
4. Start the sauce: Turn the heat to medium. If the skillet is dry, add a little more olive oil. Add the anchovy filets. Cook for about 2 minutes or so, pushing the anchovies around the skillet. They will kind of melt into the oil and infuse it with flavor.
5. Finish the sauce: Add the garlic and cook until fragrant, about 30 seconds. Add the tomatoes, half of the olives, half of the capers, and the dried oregano and red pepper flakes (if using). Bring the sauce to a simmer over medium heat.
6. Cook the chicken in the sauce: Add the chicken back into the skillet, nestling it in the sauce. Spoon a bit of the sauce over the chicken. Cover part way, either with a lid or a splatter guard. Cook until the chicken is fully cooked and tender, about 25-30 minutes, depending on how large the pieces are. A thermometer in the thickest part of the chicken should read 165°F.
7. Serve: Garnish with the parsley and the remaining olives and capers and serve.

Nutritional Value (Amount per Serving):

Calories: 584; Fat: 44.35; Carb: 5.01; Protein: 39.64

Cashew Mango Grilled Chicken

Prep Time: 10 Minutes   Cook Time: 15 Minutes   Serves: 8

Ingredients:

- 1/4 cup mango chutney, chopped
- 1/4 cup cashew butter
- 2 tablespoons reduced-sodium soy sauce
- 2 tablespoons rice vinegar
- 8 boneless skinless chicken thighs
- 1/2 teaspoon salt
- 1/2 teaspoon crushed red pepper flakes
- 1 large mango, peeled and thinly sliced
- 1/3 cup lightly salted cashews, chopped
- Additional mango chutney, optional

Directions:

1. Mix together first 4 ingredients until blended.
2. Sprinkle chicken with salt and pepper flakes; place on an oiled grill rack over medium heat. Grill chicken, covered, until a thermometer reads 170°F, 6-8 minutes per side, brushing with chutney mixture during the last

5 minutes. Serve with mango; top with cashews and, if desired, additional chutney.

Nutritional Value (Amount per Serving):

Calories: 464; Fat: 18.6; Carb: 17.6; Protein: 55.46

Lemon Rosemary Chicken

Prep Time: 5 Minutes   Cook Time: 20 Minutes   Serves: 6

Ingredients:

- 1 ½ pounds boneless skinless chicken breasts, about 3 chicken breasts
- Kosher salt
- Black pepper
- Extra virgin olive oil
- 2 lemons, divided
- ¼ cup chicken broth
- 2 tablespoons chopped fresh rosemary
- 4 large garlic cloves, minced
- 1 medium yellow onion, halved and sliced (half moons)

Directions:

1. Prep the oven: Preheat the oven to 400°F and position a rack in the middle.
2. Slice the breasts into cutlets: Place the chicken breast flat on a cutting board and position your non-dominant hand on top to hold it firmly. Using a sharp knife, in your dominant hand, carefully slice the chicken breast horizontally starting with the thicker end and all the way through to the thin end. You should end up with two thinner cutlets for each chicken breast half. If the cutlets still need to flatten a bit, cover with plastic wrap and pound with a kitchen mallet (optional).
3. Dry and season the chicken: Pat the chicken breast cutlets dry and season with kosher salt and black pepper on both sides.
4. Prepare the baking dish: In a 9x13 baking dish, add about 3 tablespoons extra virgin olive oil, juice of 1 lemon (leave the second lemon for later), chicken broth, rosemary, and the minced garlic. Mix to combine.
5. Add the chicken cutlets: Add the chicken breast cutlets to the baking dish and toss to coat with the olive oil and garlic mixture, then add the onion slices and toss again. Cover the baking dish with a large piece of foil, making sure the foil is not touching the chicken.
6. Bake: Place the covered dish on the middle rack of your heated oven for 10 minutes, then carefully remove the foil and return the baking dish back to the oven for another 10 to 15 minutes or until the chicken is fully cooked and is no longer pink in the middle. Remove the chicken from the oven when the internal temperature reaches 160°F. Cover and let rest for another 5 minutes and the chicken will come up to 165°F. Cut half of the

remaining lemon into slices to garnish the chicken. Squeeze the juice from the other half over the chicken and it's ready to eat!

Nutritional Value (Amount per Serving):

Calories: 170; Fat: 4.76; Carb: 2.41; Protein: 27.96

Mediterranean Chickpea And Chicken Soup

Prep Time: 25 Minutes   Cook Time: 25 Minutes   Serves: 4 To 6

Ingredients:
- 1 large yellow onion
- 1 large yellow, red, or orange bell pepper
- 4 cloves garlic
- 1 teaspoon smoked paprika
- 1/2 teaspoon ground cumin
- 1/2 teaspoon kosher salt
- 2 (15-ounce) cans chickpeas
- 4 boneless, skinless chicken
- thighs (about 2 pounds total)
- 3 tablespoons olive oil
- 1 (32-ounce) box low-sodium chicken broth
- 1 (15-ounce) can diced tomatoes
- 2 tablespoons tomato paste
- 5 ounces baby spinach (about 5 cups)

Directions:

1. Prepare the following, placing them together in a medium bowl: Dice 1 large yellow onion and 1 large bell pepper, and mince 4 garlic cloves. Combine 1 teaspoon smoked paprika, 1/2 teaspoon ground cumin, and 1/2 teaspoon kosher salt in a small bowl. Drain and rinse 2 cans chickpeas.
2. Pat 4 boneless skinless chicken thighs dry with paper towels. Sprinkle all over with the spice mixture.
3. Heat 3 tablespoons olive oil in a large pot over medium-high heat until shimmering. Add the onion, pepper, and garlic, and cook until softened, about 3 minutes. Push the vegetables to one side of the pot and add the chicken to the other side. Add 1 box chicken broth and the chickpeas. Bring the mixture to a simmer. Cover and simmer, reducing the heat as needed, until the chicken and chickpeas are tender, 22 to 25 minutes.
4. Transfer the chicken to a clean cutting board. Add 1 can diced tomatoes and their juices and 2 tablespoons tomato paste to the soup and stir to combine well. Use a fork to shred the chicken into bite-sized pieces, then return the chicken to the pot. Simmer for 5 minutes more.
5. Remove the pot from the heat. Add 5 ounces baby spinach (about 5 cups) and stir until the spinach is wilted. Serve immediately.

Nutritional Value (Amount per Serving):

Calories: 321; Fat: 13.34; Carb: 31.03; Protein: 21.98

Sheet-Pan Chicken Thighs with Brussels Sprouts Gnocchi

Prep Time: 20 Minutes   Cook Time: 20 Minutes   Serves: 4

Ingredients:

- 4 tablespoons extra-virgin olive oil, divided
- 2 tablespoons chopped fresh oregano, divided
- 2 large cloves garlic, minced, divided
- ½ teaspoon ground pepper, divided
- ¼ teaspoon salt, divided
- 1 pound Brussels sprouts, trimmed and quartered
- 1 (16 ounce) package shelf-stable gnocchi
- 1 cup sliced red onion
- 4 boneless, skinless chicken thighs, trimmed
- 1 cup halved cherry tomatoes
- 1 tablespoon red-wine vinegar

Directions:

1. Preheat oven to 450 degrees F.
2. Stir 2 tablespoons oil, 1 tablespoon oregano, half the garlic, 1/4 teaspoon pepper and 1/8 teaspoon salt together in a large bowl. Add Brussels sprouts, gnocchi and onion; toss to coat. Spread on a large rimmed baking sheet.
3. Stir 1 tablespoon oil, the remaining 1 tablespoon oregano, the remaining garlic and the remaining 1/4 teaspoon pepper and 1/8 teaspoon salt in the large bowl. Add chicken and toss to coat. Nestle the chicken into the vegetable mixture. Roast for 10 minutes.
4. Remove from the oven and add the tomatoes; stir to combine. Continue roasting until the Brussels sprouts are tender and the chicken is just cooked through, about 10 minutes more. Stir vinegar and the remaining 1 tablespoon oil into the vegetable mixture.

Nutritional Value (Amount per Serving):

Calories: 785; Fat: 21.83; Carb: 79.29; Protein: 67.72

Chapter 7: Beef, Pork, and Lamb

Moroccan Apple Beef Stew

Prep Time: 20 Minutes   Cook Time: 2 Hours   Serves: 8

Ingredients:

- 1-1/4 teaspoons salt
- 1/2 teaspoon ground cinnamon
- 1/2 teaspoon pepper
- 1/4 teaspoon ground allspice
- 2-1/2 pounds beef stew meat, cut into 1-inch pieces
- 2 to 3 tablespoons olive oil
- 1 large onion, chopped (about 2 cups)
- 3 garlic cloves, minced
- 1 can (15 ounces) tomato sauce
- 1 can (14-1/2 ounces) beef broth
- 1 cup pitted dried plums (prunes), coarsely chopped
- 1 tablespoon honey
- 2 medium Fuji or Gala apples, peeled and cut into 1-1/2-inch pieces
- Hot cooked rice or couscous, optional

Directions:

1. Mix salt, cinnamon, pepper and allspice; sprinkle over beef and toss to coat. In a Dutch oven, heat 2 tablespoons oil over medium heat.
2. Brown beef in batches, adding more oil as necessary. Remove beef with a slotted spoon.
3. Add onion to same pan; cook and stir until tender, 6-8 minutes. Add garlic; cook 1 minute longer. Stir in tomato sauce, broth, dried plums and honey. Return beef to pan; bring to a boil. Reduce heat; simmer, covered, 1-1/2 hours.
4. Add apples; cook, covered, until beef and apples are tender, 30-45 minutes longer. Skim fat. If desired, serve stew with rice or couscous.

Nutritional Value (Amount per Serving):

Calories: 416; Fat: 15.89; Carb: 19.42; Protein: 50.33

Braised Lamb Chops With Cranberry-Harissa

Prep Time: 10 Minutes   Cook Time: 2 Hours 25 Minutes   Serves: 4-6

Ingredients:

- ain Ingredients
- 8 lamb chops (2-inch thick)
- olive oil
- 1 large shallot, thinly sliced
- 1 cup dry white wine
- 1 bay leaf
- 1/2 lemon, juice of
- 2 cups broth (your choice of beef or vegetable broth)
- Fresh parsley for garnish
- pice Mix
- 1/2 tsp salt
- 1 tsp black pepper
- 1 tsp garlic powder

- 2 tsp dried crushed mint (more for garnish)
- ranberry-Harissa And Mint Chutney
- 2 cups cranberries
- 1/2 cup brown sugar
- 1/2 tsp fresh chopped rosemary
- 1 tsp dried crushed mint
- 1/2 lemon, juice of
- 1 tsp fresh grated ginger
- 1 cup water, more if needed
- 1 tsp harissa paste

Directions:

1. Preheat oven to 350 degrees F.
2. Prepare the spice mix.
3. Spice the lamb chops on all sides generously with the spice mix.
4. In a large cast iron skillet, heat 2 tbsp olive oil. Now add lamb chops and brown on all sides over medium-high heat.
5. Remove lamb momentarily from the cooking skillet.
6. In the same skillet, add sliced shallots and toss around briefly. Now add white wine and bay leaf. Bring to a high simmer and let the liquid reduce slightly (about 4 minutes). Add broth and lemon juice, and let simmer again on medium-high heat for another 5 minutes.
7. Add lamb back to skillet and let everything cook together for 10 minutes.
8. Cover skillet and place in a 350 F-heated oven for 1 1/2 hours to 2 hours, or until lamb is cooked to tender. Turn lamb over half-way through cooking. Uncover and let cook another 10 minutes.
9. While lamb cooks, proceed to make the cranberry-harissa and mint chutney. Place chutney ingredients in a heavy sauce pan or pot. Place on medium-high heat and bring to a boil; stirring occasionally. Reduce heat to medium-low; cover and let simmer until cranberries soften forming a thick chutney (about 10-15 minutes). Stir a couple of times while it cooks. Remove from heat and set aside.
10. Once lamb is ready, serve hot with a little garnish of crushed mint and fresh parsley leaves. Place wine-lemon braising sauce and the cranberry-harissa chutney in two bowls to serve alongside the lamb.

Nutritional Value (Amount per Serving):

Calories: 650; Fat: 45.96; Carb: 26.17; Protein: 31.78

Pork Chops With Bay Leaf And Lemon Slices

Prep Time: 10 Minutes   Cook Time: 20 Minutes   Serves: 4

Ingredients:
- 2 tablespoons extra-virgin olive oil
- 3 garlic cloves, thinly sliced
- 4 fresh or dried bay leaves

- 1 lemon, thinly sliced
- 4 bone-in center-cut pork chops, 6 to 8 ounces each
- 1 to 1 ½ teaspoons fine salt
- Freshly ground black pepper to taste
- ¼ cup dry white wine

Directions:

1. Heat the Oil and Aromatics: In a large cast-iron or heavy-bottomed stainless-steel skillet set over medium-low heat, place 2 tablespoons extra-virgin olive oil, sliced garlic, and bay leaves. Cook, stirring, until the garlic is lightly golden, and the oil is infused with the aroma of garlic and bay leaf, about 5 minutes. Transfer the garlic and bay leaves to a plate and set aside. Leave the oil in the pan.
2. Cook the sliced lemon: Add the lemon slices to the pan and cook for about 2 minutes to brown the bottom. The juice from the lemon slices can cause the fat in the pan to spatter, so watch out and turn down the heat if necessary. Once the slices are browned on the bottom, turn them with tongs or a fork and brown the other side. Transfer the browned lemon slices to the plate with the garlic and bay leaves.
3. Season and pan-sear the pork chops: Season the pork chops on both sides with salt and pepper. Arrange them in the pan, taking care not to crowd them or they won't brown properly. Brown them two at a time if necessary. Raise the heat to medium-high and sear the chops until nicely browned on the bottom, 2 to 3 minutes. Turn the chops and cook until browned on the other side, 2 to 3 minutes.
4. Add the wine: Pour in the wine and let it bubble for about 30 seconds. Then lower then heat to medium-low and return the garlic, bay leaves, and lemon slices to the pan. Cook the pork chops for another 3 to 5 minutes, or until an instant-read meat thermometer inserted in the center of the chop registers 145°F.
5. Serve: Transfer the pork chops to a serving platter and spoon the pan juices, along with the lemon slices, over the top. Let sit for just a minute or two to rest before serving.

Nutritional Value (Amount per Serving):

Calories: 321; Fat: 21.82; Carb: 1.7; Protein: 28.04

Mediterranean Meatball Bowls

Prep Time: 20 Minutes   Cook Time: 30 Minutes   Serves: 4

Ingredients:

- 1 cup uncooked farro
- 3 cups water or broth

- 1 lb ground beef (I like 90/10 for meatballs)
- 2 cloves **garlic**, grated or finely minced
- ⅓ cup onion, grated or finely minced
- 1 tbsp fresh oregano, chopped (or 2 tsp dried)
- 2 tsp fresh dill, chopped (or 1 tsp dried)
- 1 tbsp red wine vinegar (or lemon juice)
- 1 tsp smoked paprika (optional)
- Pinch salt and black pepper
- 4 cups baby spinach or other leafy green
- 1 large cucumber, sliced
- 1 cup cherry tomatoes, halved
- ½ cup hummus **and/or** tzatziki sauce
- ¼ cup crumbled feta cheese
- Canned chickpeas, drained and rinsed or roasted
- Olives, fresh herbs, or any other toppings you like

Directions:

1. Heat oven to 425°F.
2. Make the meatballs by mixing together all the ingredients in a bowl. Roll them into 1 ½-inch balls and place on a baking sheet lined with parchment or in a cast iron skillet. Bake them for 15-20 minutes.
3. Ground beef should be cooked to an internal temperature of 160°F. Color is not a reliable indicator of ground beef doneness.
4. While the meatballs are baking, chop the veggies and cook your favorite whole grain. I like farro or quinoa, but you can really use any whole grain that you love. These bowls are also great for using leftover grains if you like to batch cook.
5. Once the grains and meatballs are done, assemble the bowls. Start with a bed of grains and leafy greens in each of 4 bowls, then add the meatballs, veggies, chickpeas, hummus/tzatziki and feta.

Nutritional Value (Amount per Serving):

Calories: 490; Fat: 16.94; Carb: 47.71; Protein: 39.65

Lamb Meatballs With Caramelized Onions

Prep Time: 10 Minutes   Cook Time: 45 Minutes   Serves: 24

Ingredients:

- 3 tablespoons extra virgin olive oil
- 3 medium yellow onions, sliced into ¼-inch rings
- 1 small yellow onion, grated
- Kosher salt
- 1 ½ pounds ground lamb
- ⅓ cup breadcrumbs
- ½ bunch fresh parsley, leaves chopped
- 1 egg
- 2 garlic cloves, minced

- 1 ½ teaspoons Baharat
- ¼ teaspoon ground cardamom

- Black pepper

Directions:

1. Heat your oven: Preheat your oven to 425°F.
2. Caramelize the sliced onions: In a large oven-safe pan over medium-high heat, add the olive oil. Once it shimmers. Add the sliced onion rings and season with a big pinch of salt. Cook, stirring occasionally, until the onions have fully softened and turned a deep golden brown, 20-30 minutes.
3. Make the meatballs: While the onions are cooking, combine the grated onion, lamb, breadcrumbs, parsley, egg, garlic, Baharat, and cardamom in a large mixing bowl. Add a big pinch of kosher salt and black pepper and mix to combine. Take handfuls of the meat mixture (about 2 tablespoons each) and form them into meatballs. You should end up with about 18-20 meatballs.
4. Make the onion sauce: When the onions are ready, turn off the heat and carefully stir in 1 cup of water. The water should turn brown immediately. Nestle the lamb meatballs into the onion sauce, and using a spoon, scoop some of the onions on top.
5. Bake the meatballs: Transfer the pan to the oven to bake on the center rack until the meatballs are cooked through and no longer pink in the middle, about 25 to 30 minutes. I like to occasionally baste the meatballs with the onion sauce while they bake.
6. Serve: Spoon the meatballs, onions, and sauce over Basmati Rice or Rice with Vermicelli. Enjoy!

Nutritional Value (Amount per Serving):

Calories: 71; Fat: 4.71; Carb: 0.86; Protein: 6.29

Perfect Roasted Leg Of Lamb

Prep Time: 1 Hour   Cook Time: 1 Hour 25 Minutes   Serves: 8

Ingredients:

- 1 4 to 5 pound leg of lamb, bone-in, fat trimmed
- Salt and pepper
- Extra virgin olive oil
- 5 garlic cloves, peeled and sliced; more for later
- 2 cups water
- 8 gold potatoes, peeled and cut into wedges

- 1 yellow onion, peeled and cut into wedges
- 1 teaspoon paprika, more for later
- 1 teaspoon all-natural garlic powder
- Fresh parsley for garnish, optional
- or The Rub:
- 15 garlic cloves, peeled
- 2 tablespoons dried oregano

- 2 tablespoons dried mint flakes
- 1 tablespoons paprika
- ½ tablespoons nutmeg
- ½ cup Extra virgin olive oil
- 2 lemons, juice of

Directions:

1. Bring the leg of lamb to room temp. Take the leg of lamb out of the refrigerator and leave in room temperature for about 1 hour. In the meantime, prepare the remaining ingredients and make the lamb rub.
2. Prepare the seasoning. To make the rub or seasoning, in a food processor, combine the rub ingredients. Blend until smooth. Set aside (or in the fridge, if preparing in advance).
3. Salt the meat. When ready, pat the lamb dry and make a few slits on both sides. Season with salt and pepper.
4. Sear the Lamb. Turn the oven on broil. Place the leg of lamb on a wire rack and put it directly on the top rack so that it's only a few inches away from the broiler element. Broil for 5-7 minutes on each side or until the leg of lamb is nicely seared. Remove from the oven, then adjust the oven temperature to 325 degrees F.
5. Apply the seasoning or rub. When the lamb is cool enough to handle, insert the garlic slices in the slits you made earlier. Now cover the leg of lamb on all sides with the wet rub and place it in the middle of a roasting pan with an inside rack. Add two cups of water to the bottom of the roasting pan.

For Medium Roasted Lamb Leg

1. Season the potato and onion wedges with the paprika, garlic powder and a little salt, then add them to the pan on either side of the lamb.
2. Cover and roast. Tent a large piece of foil over the roasting pan (make sure it does not touch the lamb) then place the pan on the middle rack of the 325 degrees F heated-oven. Roast covered for about 1 hour. Remove the foil and return the roasting pan to the oven for another 15 to 20 minutes or until the lamb temperature registers 125 degrees F.
3. Let rest. Remove the pan from the oven and let the leg of lamb rest for about 15 to 20 minutes before serving (the lamb will continue to cook and its internal temperature will continue to rise to around 130 degrees F).
4. Serve. Place the roast lamb and potatoes in a large serving platter over a bed of rice, you like. Garnish with parsley. Or, you may carve the lamb first, then arrange the sliced lamb with the potatoes over the rice.

Nutritional Value (Amount per Serving):

Calories: 710; Fat: 20.64; Carb: 75.46; Protein: 55.35

Greek Lamb Souvlaki Skewers

Prep Time: 35 Minutes   Cook Time: 25 Minutes   Serves: 6

Ingredients:

- 1 lb. lamb leg or shoulder, cut into 1.5-inch cubes
- 1/3 cup olive oil, divided
- 1 tablespoon lemon juice, freshly squeezed
- 2 tablespoons garlic, minced
- 2 tablespoons Italian seasoning
- 1 tablespoon cumin powder
- 2 teaspoons salt (or to taste)
- 1 tablespoon ground black pepper

Directions:

1. Marinate the lamb. Add cubed lamb into a zip-loc bag, and add 1/4 cup olive oil, lemon juice, minced garlic, Italian seasoning, cumin, salt and pepper. Press the air out of the bag and seal tightly. Press the marinade around the lamb to coat. Place in the fridge to marinate at least 30 minutes or overnight, to infuse all the seasoning and spices into the meat.
2. Skewer the lamb. Thread the lamb onto skewers, and lightly brush some olive oil.
3. Grill the skewers. Preheat a grill pan over medium high heat for 4-5 minutes and lightly brush the grill with remaining olive oil. You should notice the oil shimmer and sizzle when it's hot and ready. Grill the lamb skewers for 8-10 minutes on each side or until the internal temperature for the lamb reaches 155 F. For well done, cook 1-2 more minutes on each side or until the internal temperature reaches above 160 F.

Nutritional Value (Amount per Serving):

Calories: 227; Fat: 16.16; Carb: 3.94; Protein: 15.28

Slow Cooker Carnitas (Pulled Pork)

Prep Time: 10 Minutes   Cook Time: 25 Minutes   Serves: 4-6

Ingredients:

- 3 lb. boneless pork shoulder or baby back ribs (2 racks)
- 1 tablespoon vegetable oil
- 2 teaspoons salt
- 1 teaspoon ground black pepper
- 2 teaspoons dried oregano
- 1/2 teaspoon paprika
- 1/2 teaspoon garlic powder
- 1 medium onion, coarsely chopped
- 1/2 cup water
- 2 tablespoons scallions, chopped (optional, for garnish)

Directions:

1. Pat dry pork shoulder or ribs with paper towel completely and set aside.
2. In a small mixing bowl, stir well to combine oil with all the dry rub ingredients until smooth (salt, pepper, oregano, paprika, and garlic powder). Rub and spread onto pork until evenly coated.

3. Spread chopped onions evenly inside a 6-quart slow cooker (or crockpot) and add water. Place pork on top of onions. If using ribs, you can stack them on top of each other.
4. Cover and cook on 8-10 hours on the LOW setting or 4-6 hours on the HIGH setting until fork tender.
5. Shred the pork by using two forks to pull the meat apart into small bite size and discard the bones (if using ribs).
6. To crisp the shredded pork (optional), add shredded pork along with some drippings from the slow cooker into a large frying pan. Spread evenly. Heat over medium-high heat for 6-8 minutes until the juices evaporate and pork turns nicely brown and crispy.
7. Garnish with scallions and serve with Cilantro Lime Rice or Pulled Pork Tacos.

Nutritional Value (Amount per Serving):

Calories: 320; Fat: 10.06; Carb: 2.7; Protein: 51.51

Middle Eastern Ground Beef Pita Sandwich

Prep Time: 10 Minutes   Cook Time: 10 Minutes   Serves: 6

Ingredients:

- Extra virgin olive oil
- 1 medium yellow onion, chopped
- 2 garlic cloves, chopped
- 1 ½ pounds ground beef or ground turkey
- Salt and pepper
- 1 ½ teaspoon ground allspice
- ½ teaspoon cayenne pepper
- ½ teaspoon green cardamom
- ½ teaspoon ground nutmeg
- ½ teaspoon paprika
- ½ cup chopped flat-leaf parsley

- 0 Serve
- 3 Pitas, cut into halves (should make 6 pita pockets)
- 2 medium tomatoes, halved and thinly sliced
- 1 small red onion, sliced
- ½ English cucumber, halved and thinly sliced (half moons)
- 1 radish, sliced (optional)
- 1 Tahini sauce recipe, tzatziki or hummus will also work here

Directions:

1. In a large non-stick pan, heat about 2 tablespoons extra virgin olive oil over medium-high heat until shimmering. Add the onions and garlic and cook, stirring regularly, until golden brown (about 3 to 5 minutes).
2. Add the ground meat and break it up with a wooden spoon. Cook, stirring occasionally, until the meat is fully browned. Carefully drain extra fat (this is especially helpful if you did not use lean meat). Season with Kosher salt

and black pepper. Add the rest of the spices and the parsley and toss to combine.

3. To assemble the pita sandwiches, stuff each pita pocket (or pita half) with the meat mixture. Tuck slices of tomatoes, onions and cucumbers around the beef. Finish with a drizzle of tahini sauce and serve!

Nutritional Value (Amount per Serving):

Calories: 196; Fat: 9.98; Carb: 4.08; Protein: 23.26

Sheet Pan Lamb Chops

Prep Time: 25 Minutes   Cook Time: 45 Minutes   Serves: 5

Ingredients:

- or The Lamb Chops:
- 5 lamb loin chops (1.5 lbs.)
- 2 tablespoons olive oil
- 1 tablespoon salt
- 1 teaspoon ground black pepper
- 2 tablespoons garlic, minced
- 1 teaspoon fresh rosemary, finely chopped
- 2 tablespoons lemon juice (approximately juice from 1/2 lemon), freshly squeezed
- 1 tablespoon Dijon mustard
- or The Vegetables:
- 2 medium russet potatoes, peeled and cut into 1-inch cubes
- 1 medium onion, sliced
- 3 medium carrots, peeled and sliced
- 1 medium zucchini, sliced
- 2 tablespoons fresh garlic, minced
- 2 tablespoons olive oil
- 2 tablespoons lemon juice (approximately juice from 1/2 lemon), freshly squeezed
- 1 teaspoon Italian seasoning
- 1/2 teaspoon salt (or to taste)
- 1/2 teaspoon ground black pepper (or to taste)
- 1 head of garlic, halved
- 4 sprigs fresh rosemary

Directions:

1. Preheat oven to 375 F.

Marinate The Lamb Chops:

1. Using a paper towel, pat dry the lamb chops completely and transfer into a large bowl or ziploc bag.
2. Season all sides generously with olive oil, salt and pepper. Add garlic, rosemary, lemon juice and dijon mustard and toss well to coat evenly. Set aside at room temperature for at least 20 minutes. This helps the lamb chops infuse all the flavours and cook evenly when the lamb is brought to room temperature.

Prepare The Vegetables:

1. In a large mixing bowl, add potatoes, onion, carrots, zucchini and garlic, olive oil, lemon juice, Italian seasoning, salt and pepper. Toss to combine

until well coated.
2. Arrange the vegetable mixture in a single layer on a large half sheet baking pan.

Roast:

1. Bake the vegetable mixture for 20 minutes. Remove the pan out of the oven and gently shake to ensure even cooking.
2. Arrange marinated lamb chops, head or garlic and rosemary sprigs on top. Return the pan to the oven and bake for another 25 minutes until the vegetables are tender and golden brown, and the internal temperature for the lamb chops should be about 130F as read on a meat thermometer.
3. Remove the pan out of the oven and let the lamb chops rest at room temperature for 5 minutes. Serve lamb chops with roasted vegetables.

Nutritional Value (Amount per Serving):

Calories: 399; Fat: 19.13; Carb: 31.76; Protein: 27.03

Chapter 8: Vegetable

Black Bean Hummus

Prep Time: 5 Minutes   Cook Time: 5 Minutes   Serves: 8

Ingredients:

- 1 clove garlic
- 1 (15 ounce) can black beans; drain and reserve liquid
- 2 tablespoons lemon juice
- 1 ½ tablespoons tahini
- ¾ teaspoon ground cumin
- ½ teaspoon salt
- ¼ teaspoon cayenne pepper
- ¼ teaspoon paprika
- 10 Greek olives

Directions:

1. Mince garlic in the bowl of a food processor. Add black beans, 2 tablespoons reserved liquid, 2 tablespoons lemon juice, tahini, 1/2 teaspoon cumin, 1/2 teaspoon salt, and 1/8 teaspoon cayenne pepper; process until smooth, scraping down the sides as needed. Add additional seasoning and liquid to taste. Garnish with paprika and Greek olives.

Nutritional Value (Amount per Serving):

Calories: 59; Fat: 2.6; Carb: 7.06; Protein: 2.42

Greek Lentil Soup (Fakes)

Prep Time: 10 Minutes   Cook Time: 1 Hrs   Serves: 4

Ingredients:

- 8 ounces brown lentils
- ¼ cup olive oil
- 1 medium onion, minced
- 1 large carrot, chopped
- 1 tablespoon minced garlic
- 1 quart water
- 2 bay leaves
- 1 teaspoon dried oregano
- 1 pinch crushed dried rosemary (Optional)
- 1 tablespoon tomato paste
- salt and ground black pepper to taste
- 1 teaspoon olive oil, or to taste
- 1 teaspoon red wine vinegar, or to taste (Optional)

Directions:

1. Place lentils in a large saucepan; add enough water to cover by 1 inch. Bring water to a boil and cook for 10 minutes; drain.
2. Heat olive oil in a saucepan over medium heat. Add onion, carrot, and garlic; cook and stir until onion has softened and turned translucent, about 5 minutes. Pour in lentils, then add 1 quart water, bay leaves, oregano, and rosemary. Bring to a boil. Cover and reduce heat to medium-low; simmer

for 10 minutes.

3.Stir in tomato paste; season with salt and pepper. Cover and simmer, stirring occasionally, until lentils have softened, 30 to 40 minutes. Add additional water if soup becomes too thick. Drizzle with olive oil and red wine vinegar to serve.

Nutritional Value (Amount per Serving):

Calories: 225; Fat: 15.27; Carb: 20.75; Protein: 6.21

Basic Marinara for the Instant Pot

Prep Time: 10 Minutes   Cook Time: 30 Minutes   Serves: 6

Ingredients:

- 2 tablespoons olive oil
- 1 cup diced onion
- 1 tablespoon minced garlic
- ¼ cup dry red wine
- 1 (28 ounce) can diced tomatoes
- 1 (28 ounce) can whole peeled tomatoes
- 1 tablespoon dried basil
- 1 tablespoon dried oregano
- 1 tablespoon dried parsley
- ¾ teaspoon sea salt
- freshly ground black pepper to taste
- 1 pinch red pepper flakes
- 1 bay leaf

Directions:

1.Turn on a multi-functional pressure cooker (such as Instant Pot) and select Saute function to heat the pot. Add olive oil and onion; cook until onion is translucent, 3 to 5 minutes. Add garlic and cook until fragrant, about 1 minute. Pour in red wine and simmer until reduced by half.

2.Pour diced tomatoes and whole tomatoes into the pot. Bring to a simmer. Stir in basil, oregano, parsley, salt, pepper, red pepper flakes, and bay leaf. Press Keep Warm. Close and lock the lid. Seal the vent. Select Manual function and set timer for 10 minutes. Allow 10 to 15 minutes for the pressure to build.

3.Release pressure carefully using the quick-release method according to manufacturer's instructions, about 5 minutes. Unlock and remove the lid. Discard bay leaf. Use an immersion blender to puree the sauce.

Nutritional Value (Amount per Serving):

Calories: 258; Fat: 16.58; Carb: 11.61; Protein: 15.58

Grilled Veggies with Mustard Vinaigrette

Prep Time: 20 Minutes   Cook Time: 15 Minutes   Serves: 10

Ingredients:

- 1/4 cup red wine vinegar
- 1 tablespoon Dijon mustard
- 1 tablespoon honey
- 1/2 teaspoon salt
- 1/8 teaspoon pepper
- 1/4 cup canola oil
- 1/4 cup olive oil
- egetables:

- 2 large sweet onions
- 2 medium zucchini
- 2 yellow summer squash
- 2 large sweet red peppers, halved and seeded
- 1 bunch green onions, trimmed
- Cooking spray

Directions:

1. In a small bowl, whisk the first 5 ingredients. Gradually whisk in oils until blended.
2. Peel and quarter each sweet onion, leaving root ends intact. Cut zucchini and yellow squash lengthwise into 1/2-in.-thick slices. Lightly spritz onions, zucchini, yellow squash and remaining vegetables with cooking spray, turning to coat all sides.
3. Grill sweet onions, covered, over medium heat 15-20 minutes until tender, turning occasionally. Grill zucchini, squash and peppers, covered, over medium heat 10-15 minutes or until crisp-tender and lightly charred, turning once. Grill green onions, covered, 2-4 minutes or until lightly charred, turning once.
4. Cut vegetables into bite-sized pieces; place in a large bowl. Add 1/2 cup vinaigrette and toss to coat. Serve with remaining vinaigrette.

Nutritional Value (Amount per Serving):

Calories: 158; Fat: 12.49; Carb: 11.08; Protein: 1.42

Easy 20-Minute One Pot Lentils

Prep Time: 10 Minutes   Cook Time: 20 Minutes   Serves: 4-6

Ingredients:

- 1 1/2 cups dry brown lentils
- 1 teaspoon olive oil
- 1/2 cup onion, chopped
- 1 clove garlic, minced
- 1/4 teaspoon turmeric
- 3 cups boiling water, divided

- 1/2 teaspoon ground cumin
- 1/2 teaspoon Italian seasoning
- 1/2 teaspoon salt
- 1/4 teaspoon ground black pepper
- fresh cilantro, chopped (optional, for serving)

Directions:

1. Add lentils to a large mixing bowl and sort out any debris, then rinse and

drain. Pour in some boiling water on top, enough to cover the lentils, and let it sit for 10 minutes. Set aside.

2. Meanwhile, in a large pot or 4 quart Dutch oven, heat oil over medium heat. Add onions, garlic, and turmeric. Sauté until the onions are soft and translucent, about 2-3 minutes. Pour in 1 cup of boiling water into the pot and stir together.

3. Drain the lentils that have been soaking in water, then rinse and drain again. Stir the lentils into the pot along with the remaining 2 cups boiling water, cumin, Italian seasoning, salt, and pepper. Turn the heat up to high and bring to a boil. Then, turn to low and simmer covered for 15 minutes.

4. Season with more salt and pepper to taste. Serve over brown or white rice, coconut rice, or a rice pilaf with a sprinkle of fresh cilantro on top. You can also serve on its own with a naan bread, pita bread, biscuits or dinner rolls for dipping.

Nutritional Value (Amount per Serving):

Calories: 102; Fat: 3.12; Carb: 15.71; Protein: 2.79

Slow-Cooker Mediterranean Diet Stew

Prep Time: 15 Minutes   Cook Time: 6 Hours 30 Minutes   Serves: 6

Ingredients:

- 2 (14 ounce) cans no-salt-added fire-roasted diced tomatoes
- 3 cups low-sodium vegetable broth
- 1 cup coarsely chopped onion
- ¾ cup chopped carrot
- 4 cloves garlic, minced
- 1 teaspoon dried oregano
- ¾ teaspoon salt
- ½ teaspoon crushed red pepper
- ¼ teaspoon ground pepper
- 1 (15 ounce) can no-salt-added chickpeas, rinsed, divided
- 1 bunch lacinato kale, stemmed and chopped (about 8 cups)
- 1 tablespoon lemon juice
- 3 tablespoons extra-virgin olive oil
- Fresh basil leaves, torn if large
- 6 lemon wedges (Optional)

Directions:

1. Combine tomatoes, broth, onion, carrot, garlic, oregano, salt, crushed red pepper and pepper in a 4-quart slow cooker. Cover and cook on Low for 6 hours.

2. Measure 1/4 cup of the cooking liquid from the slow cooker into a small bowl. Add 2 tablespoons chickpeas; mash with a fork until smooth.

3. Add the mashed chickpeas, kale, lemon juice and remaining whole chickpeas to the mixture in the slow cooker. Stir to combine. Cover and

cook on Low until the kale is tender, about 30 minutes.

4. Ladle the stew evenly into 6 bowls; drizzle with oil. Garnish with basil. Serve with lemon wedges, if desired.

Nutritional Value (Amount per Serving):

Calories: 192; Fat: 5.38; Carb: 32.32; Protein: 8.01

Brothy Tuscan White Beans With Garlic-Fried Bread

Prep Time: 5 Minutes   Cook Time: 35 Minutes   Serves: 4

Ingredients:

- 2 (about 15-ounce) cans white beans
- 5 cloves garlic, divided
- 1/4 cup plus 2 tablespoons olive oil, divided, plus more for serving
- 6 fresh sage leaves
- 1/4 teaspoon red pepper flakes, plus more for serving
- 2 cups low-sodium vegetable broth, chicken broth, or water
- 1 (about 14-ounce) can cherry or

- diced tomatoes
- 1/2 teaspoon kosher salt, plus more as needed
- 1/4 teaspoon freshly ground black pepper
- 4 thick slices crusty sourdough bread
- Flaky salt (optional)
- 1 tablespoon red wine vinegar
- Shaved Parmesan cheese, for serving

Directions:

1. Drain and rinse 2 cans white beans. Smash and peel 5 garlic cloves.
2. Heat 1/4 cup of the olive oil in a large pot or Dutch oven over medium heat until shimmering. Add 4 of the garlic cloves, 6 fresh sage leaves, and 1/4 teaspoon red pepper flakes. Cook, stirring occasionally, until the oil is very fragrant and the garlic is lightly browned, 2 to 3 minutes.
3. Add 2 cups low-sodium vegetable broth, chicken broth, or water, and 1 can cherry or diced tomatoes and their juices. Add the white beans, season with 1/2 teaspoon kosher salt and 1/4 teaspoon black pepper, and stir to combine. Bring to a boil over high heat.
4. Reduce the heat to low. Simmer gently, uncovered and stirring occasionally, until the flavors meld and the liquid reduces slightly, about 30 minutes. Toast the bread about 15 minutes into the simmering time.
5. Heat 1 tablespoon of the olive oil in a large cast iron or regular skillet over medium heat until shimmering. Add 2 slices of the sourdough bread and cook until golden-brown and crisp, 2 to 3 minutes per side. Transfer each slice to individual shallow bowls. Repeat with the remaining 1 tablespoon olive oil and 2 bread slices. Rub the fried bread all over with the reserved

garlic clove and sprinkle with a pinch of flaky or kosher salt.

6. Remove the beans from the heat. Stir in 1 tablespoon red wine vinegar. Taste and season with kosher salt as needed.
7. Ladle the brothy beans over the fried bread. Garnish with shaved Parmesan cheese, a drizzle of olive oil, and if desired, a pinch of red pepper flakes.

Nutritional Value (Amount per Serving):

Calories: 278; Fat: 19.41; Carb: 18.47; Protein: 8.93

Roasted Mixed Mushroom And Garlic Farrotto

Prep Time: 10-15 Minutes   Cook Time: 1 Hour 5-10 Minutes   Serves: 4

Ingredients:

- 1 medium head garlic
- 1 pound fresh mixed mushrooms, such as cremini, shiitake, and/or oyster
- 3 tablespoons plus 1 teaspoon olive oil, divided
- 2 cups semi-pearled or pearled farro
- 1 teaspoon kosher salt, divided, plus more for seasoning
- 1/2 teaspoon freshly ground black pepper, divided
- 4 cups (32 ounces) low-sodium chicken or vegetable broth
- 1 medium shallot
- 2 tablespoons fresh thyme leaves, divided
- 2 ounces Pecorino Romano cheese (about 1 packed cup grated), divided
- 1/2 cup dry white wine
- 1 tablespoon unsalted butter

Directions:

1. Arrange 2 racks to divide the oven into thirds and heat the oven to 400°F.
2. Peel off and discard the excess papery skins from 1 medium head garlic, then slice a thin layer off the top to expose the cloves. Place on a piece of aluminum foil. Drizzle with 1 teaspoon of the olive oil and sprinkle with a pinch of kosher salt. Wrap the garlic completely in the foil. Roast on the upper rack of the oven for 25 minutes. Meanwhile, remove and trim the stems from 1 pound mushrooms if needed. If not already sliced, tear the caps into bite-sized pieces and place on a rimmed baking sheet.
3. Drizzle the mushrooms with 2 tablespoons of the olive oil, and sprinkle with 1/2 teaspoon of the kosher salt and 1/4 teaspoon of the black pepper. Toss to coat, then spread out in an even layer. Transfer to the lower rack of the oven. Roast until the mushrooms and garlic are tender and caramelized, tossing the mushrooms halfway through, 15 to 20 minutes total.
4. While the mushrooms are roasting, bring a large pot of salted water to a boil. Rinse and drain 2 cups farro. Add the farro to boiling water and cook

until tender but still firm to the bite (it should not be fully cooked at this stage), 15 to 20 minutes. Meanwhile, place 4 cups broth in a small saucepan and bring to a simmer over medium heat. Reduce the heat and maintain a bare simmer. Mince 1 medium shallot and coarsely chop 2 tablespoons fresh thyme leaves. Finely grate 2 ounces Pecorino Romano cheese (about 1 packed cup); set aside.

5. Once the mushrooms and garlic are roasted, remove from the oven and set aside until the garlic is cool enough to handle, about 5 minutes. Squeeze the cloves out of their skins into a small bowl. Mash with a fork until you have a mostly smooth purée (a few lumps are okay).

6. Drain the farro. Return the now-empty pot to medium heat and add the remaining 1 tablespoon olive oil. Add the shallot and half of the thyme and sauté until the shallot is softened and translucent, 2 to 3 minutes. Add the farro, remaining 1/2 teaspoon kosher salt, and remaining 1/4 teaspoon black pepper. Cook, stirring often, until the grains smell lightly toasted, about 1 minute.

7. Add 1/2 cup dry white wine and simmer, stirring constantly and scraping up any browned bits from the bottom of the pan with a wooden spoon, until the wine has evaporated and the pot is almost dry, about 1 minute. Incrementally add the broth about 1/2 cup at a time. Simmer, stirring constantly, and wait until the liquid has been almost completely absorbed before adding the next ladle. Continue adding the broth until the farro is al dente and the broth is creamy, 8 to 10 minutes total (you likely will not use up all the broth).

8. Remove the pan from the heat. Add the roasted mushrooms, garlic purée, 1 tablespoon unsalted butter, and half of the grated cheese. Serve immediately, with the remaining grated cheese and thyme sprinkled on top of each bowl.

Nutritional Value (Amount per Serving):

Calories: 815; Fat: 31.82; Carb: 116.56; Protein: 33.58

Chapter 9: Snacks and Appetizers

Watermelon Cups

Prep Time: 25 Minutes   Cook Time: 0 Minute   Serves: 16

Ingredients:
- 16 seedless watermelon cubes (1 inch)
- 1/3 cup finely chopped cucumber
- 5 teaspoons finely chopped red onion
- 2 teaspoons minced fresh mint
- 2 teaspoons minced fresh cilantro
- 1/2 to 1 teaspoon lime juice

Directions:
1. Using a small melon baller or measuring spoon, scoop out the center of each watermelon cube, leaving a 1/4-in. shell (save centers for another use).
2. In a small bowl, combine the remaining ingredients; spoon into watermelon cubes.

Nutritional Value (Amount per Serving):

Calories: 25; Fat: 0.6; Carb: 4.25; Protein: 0.9

Oven Fried Halloumi Bites with Hot Honey

Prep Time: 15 Minutes   Cook Time: 20 Minutes   Serves: 8

Ingredients:
- 2 large eggs, beaten
- 2 (8 ounce) blocks halloumi cheese, cubed
- 1 cup Panko bread crumbs
- 1/2 cup grated parmesan
- 3 tablespoons sesame seeds
- 1/2 teaspoon paprika
- black pepper
- extra virgin olive oil
- ot Honey
- 1/3 cup honey
- red pepper flakes

Directions:
1. Preheat the oven to 425° F. Line a baking sheet with parchment paper.
2. Whisk the eggs in a bowl, add the halloumi and toss to coat. In a separate bowl, combine the panko, parmesan, sesame seeds, paprika, and a pinch of pepper.
3. Remove each piece of halloumi from the eggs, and dredge through the crumbs, tossing to coat. Place on the prepared baking sheet. Repeat until all the halloumi has been used. Make sure not to crowd your pan. Lightly drizzle the halloumi with olive oil. Bake for 10-12 minutes, then flip and bake another 10 minutes, until golden and crisp all around.

4. Meanwhile, combine the honey and a big pinch of chili flakes and sea salt.
5. Serve the halloumi warm, drizzled with the hot honey. I love a side of ketchup as well!

Nutritional Value (Amount per Serving):

Calories: 216; Fat: 11.45; Carb: 20.39; Protein: 9.46

Grilled Caprese Skewers with Halloumi and Sourdough

Prep Time: 25 Minutes   Cook Time: 1 Hour 5 Minutes   Serves: 4-6

Ingredients:
- arlic Oil
- ⅓cup extra-virgin olive oil
- 3 garlic cloves, thinly sliced
- kewers
- 3 cups sourdough bread, cubed
- 3 cups cubed halloumi
- 4 cups cherry tomatoes
- Salt and freshly ground black pepper
- ¾ cup basil leaves
- Balsamic vinegar, as needed

Directions:

1. MAKE THE GARLIC OIL: Combine the oil and garlic and heat gently over medium-low heat for 2 to 3 minutes. Let cool completely and then remove the garlic from the oil.
2. MAKE THE SKEWERS: Arrange 2 or 3 pieces of bread, 3 or 4 pieces of cheese and 3 or 4 tomatoes on each skewer. Repeat until all the skewers are assembled.
3. Brush the skewers with the garlic oil on both sides and season with salt and pepper. Working in batches, cook on a preheated grill or grill pan until nicely charred on both sides, 2 to 3 minutes per side.
4. Add a few basil leaves to the end of each skewer and then roughly chop the remaining basil and garnish the skewers with the chopped basil.
5. Serve the skewers immediately, drizzled with balsamic vinegar.

Nutritional Value (Amount per Serving):

Calories: 505; Fat: 16.56; Carb: 28.43; Protein: 58.7

Grilled Watermelon Gazpacho

Prep Time: 10 Minutes   Cook Time: 10 Minutes   Serves: 4

Ingredients:
- 2 tablespoons olive oil, divided
- 1/4 seedless watermelon, cut into

three 1-1/2-in.-thick slices
- 1 large beefsteak tomato, halved
- 1/2 English cucumber, peeled and halved lengthwise
- 1 jalapeno pepper, seeded and halved lengthwise
- 1/4 cup plus 2 tablespoons diced

red onion, divided
- 2 tablespoons sherry vinegar
- 1 tablespoon lime juice
- 1/2 teaspoon kosher or sea salt
- 1/4 teaspoon pepper
- 1 small ripe avocado, peeled, pitted and diced

Directions:

1. Brush 1 tablespoon olive oil over watermelon slices, tomato, cucumber and jalapeno; grill, covered, on a greased grill rack over medium-high direct heat until seared, 5-6 minutes on each side. Remove from heat, reserving one watermelon slice.

2. When cool enough to handle, remove rind from remaining watermelon slices; cut flesh into chunks. Remove skin and seeds from tomato and jalapeno; chop. Coarsely chop cucumber. Combine grilled vegetables; add 1/4 cup onion, vinegar, lime juice and seasonings. Process in batches in a blender until smooth, adding remaining olive oil during final minute. If desired, strain through a fine-mesh strainer; adjust seasonings as needed. Refrigerate, covered, until chilled.

3. To serve, pour gazpacho into bowls or glasses. Top with diced avocado and remaining onion. Cut reserved watermelon slice into wedges. Garnish bowls or glasses with wedges.

Nutritional Value (Amount per Serving):

Calories: 159; Fat: 14.28; Carb: 8.21; Protein: 1.74

Jessica'S Marinated Chickpeas

Prep Time: 15 Minutes   Cook Time: 0 Minute   Serves: 6

Ingredients:

- 2 cans (15 ounces each) chickpeas, rinsed and drained, or 3 cups cooked chickpeas
- 2/3 cup chopped roasted red peppers (I used most of a 12-ounce jar)
- 2/3 cup crumbled feta cheese
- 1/2 cup chopped fresh basil
- 1/3 cup olive oil
- 1/4 cup red wine vinegar

- 1 tablespoon + 1 teaspoon honey
- 4 medium cloves garlic, pressed or minced
- 1/2 teaspoon dried oregano
- 1/2 teaspoon salt
- 1/2 teaspoon freshly ground black pepper
- 1/2 teaspoon red pepper flakes (scale back significantly if sensitive to spice)

Directions:

1. In a medium serving bowl, combine the chickpeas, red peppers, feta and basil.
2. In a small bowl, whisk together the olive oil, vinegar, honey, garlic, oregano, salt, pepper and red pepper flakes.
3. Pour the dressing over the chickpeas and stir. Cover the bowl and stick it in the fridge for at least 30 minutes, for best flavor. The salad keeps for up to 5 days in the refrigerator.

Nutritional Value (Amount per Serving):

Calories: 357; Fat: 23.01; Carb: 22.85; Protein: 15.39

Maple Roasted Carrots With Yogurt Sauce

Prep Time: 10 Minutes   Cook Time: 25 Minutes   Serves: 4-6

Ingredients:

- 2 bunches carrots, peeled (about 12 carrots)
- 2 tablespoons olive oil
- 1 teaspoon salt
- 1 teaspoon cinnamon
- 1/4 teaspoon ground black pepper
- 1/4 cup maple syrup
- 1/4 cup walnuts, toasted and crushed (for garnish)

- or The Yogurt Sauce:
- 1/4 cup Greek yogurt, full-fat
- 1/2 teaspoon salt
- zest from 1 lemon
- 2 tablespoons lemon juice, freshly squeezed
- 1 tablespoon fresh tarragon, finely chopped (plus more for garnish)
- 1 tablespoon water

Directions:

1. Preheat oven to 425 F.
2. Place the carrots on a parchment-lined half sheet baking pan. Drizzle with olive oil and set aside.
3. In a small mixing bowl, combine salt, cinnamon, and pepper. Sprinkle it evenly over the carrots on all sides.
4. Roast the carrots for 20 minutes, rotating once halfway through.
5. Remove carrots from the oven and drizzle maple syrup on top. Toss to coat, then return to the oven and cook for another 5-6 minutes.
6. While carrots are cooking, make the yogurt sauce. In a small mixing bowl, combine Greek yogurt, salt, lemon zest, lemon juice, and chopped tarragon. Add water to thin it out so it's pourable. Whisk to combine, then set aside.
7. Once carrots are cooked, drizzle yogurt sauce on top, along with fresh tarragon and toasted walnuts. Serve immediately.

Nutritional Value (Amount per Serving):

Calories: 174; Fat: 9.84; Carb: 20.89; Protein: 1.98

Easy Cherry Tomato Bruschetta

Prep Time: 10 Minutes   Cook Time: 5 Minutes   Serves: 4

Ingredients:

- 4 cloves garlic (DIVIDED)
- 2 tsp olive oil (plus more for oiling pan)
- 2 cups cherry tomatoes, quartered (or other tomato of choice)
- 3 Tbsp finely chopped fresh basil
- 1/8 tsp sea salt
- 4 slices crusty bread or sourdough (or gluten-free bread as needed)

Directions:

1. To start, press (or finely mince) half of the garlic into a small mixing bowl, then add the olive oil and whisk to evenly distribute the garlic. Add the tomatoes, basil, and salt, and toss gently to combine. Set aside.
2. Generously oil a large cast iron skillet and, with the heat off, place the bread slices (as many as will fit) into the oil, then flip them to evenly coat both sides. Once the bread is oiled, turn the heat on to medium and toast the bread. Watch it closely so it doesn't burn, flipping each piece after ~2 minutes, or when the underside is deeply golden. Repeat with any remaining bread, adding more oil as needed.
3. Place your toasted bread on a wooden cutting board or other surface to cool slightly. Take your remaining cloves of garlic and cut them in half lengthwise. When the bread is cool enough to handle, rub each slice with half a clove of garlic. Finally, cut each slice of bread in half (for 8 total pieces as recipe is written // adjust if altering the default number of servings) and top each piece with a generous serving of the tomato mixture.
4. Serve immediately! Delicious alongside salads, pastas, or soups. Best when fresh, but the tomato mixture will keep for up to 2 days in the refrigerator. Not freezer friendly.

Nutritional Value (Amount per Serving):

Calories: 122; Fat: 3.07; Carb: 21.84; Protein: 2.96

Chapter 10: Desserts

Keto White Chocolate Blueberry Smoothie Bowl

Prep Time: 5 Minutes   Cook Time: 0 Minute   Serves: 1

Ingredients:

- 1 cup unsweetened milk of choice
- 1 scoop Perfect Keto Vanilla Collagen
- 2 tablespoons heavy cream
- 1/2 cup blueberries
- 1/2 tablespoon monk fruit
- 1 Perfect Keto White Chocolate Nola Bar
- 1 cup ice

Directions:

1. Add all ingredients to a high speed blender and mix on high until smooth. Add ice and blend until smoothie has thickened.
2. Pour contents into a bowl and top with crumbled Perfect Keto Nola bar, fresh blueberries, macadamia nuts, and coconut if desired.

Nutritional Value (Amount per Serving):

Calories: 1006; Fat: 58.84; Carb: 105.35; Protein: 16.21

Flourless Lemon Almond Cake

Prep Time: 20-25 Minutes   Cook Time: 25-30 Minutes   Serves: 8 To 10

Ingredients:

- Butter or cooking spray, for greasing the pan
- 4 large eggs
- 2 medium lemons
- 1/2 cup granulated sugar
- 1 1/2 cups almond flour (not almond meal)
- 1 teaspoon baking powder
- 1/2 teaspoon kosher salt
- For serving: Powdered sugar and fresh berries (optional)

Directions:

1. Arrange a rack in the middle of the oven and heat the oven to 350°F. Line the bottom of an 8- or 9-inch springform or round cake pan with parchment paper. Coat the paper and sides of the pan well with butter or cooking spray; set aside.
2. Crack and separate 4 large eggs, placing the egg whites in the bowl of a stand mixer fitted with the whisk attachment (alternatively, place in a medium bowl to and use an electric hand mixer or sturdy whisk) and the yolks in a large bowl.
3. Finely grate the zest of 2 medium lemons with a Microplane to get 2 tablespoons and place in the bowl with the egg yolks. Add 1/2 cup

granulated sugar and stir with a wooden spoon or sturdy rubber spatula until well-combined and no streaks of egg yolk remain.

4. Add 1 1/2 cups almond flour, 1 teaspoon baking powder, and 1/2 teaspoon kosher salt. Stir until the almond flour is moistened and the mixture is just combined (some lumps are fine).

5. Beat the egg whites on medium-high speed until stiff peaks form, 2 to 3 minutes (about 5 minutes by hand). Stir 1/3 of the beaten egg whites into the batter to lighten it. Then gently fold the remaining egg whites in the until just combined. The batter should be evenly moistened with no streak of egg whites remaining but will not be completely smooth; do not overmix. Transfer the batter to the prepared pan and gently spread out to an even layer.

6. Bake until the edges of the cake have begun to pull away from the sides of the pan, the top is golden brown, and a toothpick inserted into the center comes out clean, 25 to 30 minutes. Place the pan on a wire rack and let cool for 15 minutes.

7. To serve, run a knife around the cake to loosen it. Release the sides of the pan, if using a springform pan. If using a cake pan, flip the cake onto a plate, peel away the parchment, then flip it again onto a serving plate. Serve warm or at room temperature, dusting with powdered sugar and served with fresh berries, if desired.

Nutritional Value (Amount per Serving):

Calories: 72; Fat: 3.51; Carb: 8.75; Protein: 1.67

Carrot Cake Pancakes

Prep Time: 10 Minutes   Cook Time: 5 Minutes   Serves: 8-10

Ingredients:

- 1 cup all-purpose flour
- 1 tablespoon baking powder
- 1-2 tablespoons brown sugar (to taste)
- 1 teaspoon ground cinnamon
- ½ teaspoon nutmeg
- ½ teaspoon salt
- 1 cup milk, divided
- 1 large egg
- 2 tablespoons unsalted butter, melted
- ½ teaspoon vanilla extract
- 1 cup grated carrots
- vegetable oil or cooking spray

Directions:

1. In a large mixing bowl, add flour, baking powder, sugar, cinnamon, nutmeg, and salt. Whisk to combine.
2. In a medium mixing bowl, whisk together milk, egg, butter. and vanilla.

For fluffier pancakes, add just ¾ cup of milk. If the batter is too thick at the end, then mix in the remaining ¼ cup.

3. Add the wet ingredients to the dry ingredients and whisk until just combined (the batter will be slightly lumpy). Do not over mix.
4. Fold in the grated carrots.
5. Spray a large frying pan or griddle with cooking spray, or dampen a paper towel with vegetable oil and rub on top of the pan. Heat the pan over medium-low heat and add pancake batter using a ¼ measuring cup. Pour as many that will fit in your pan or griddle (I fit 3 in my 10-inch skillet).
6. Cook for 1-2 minutes until small bubbles begin to form on the surface, the edges have set, and the bottom of the pancake turns golden brown. Flip the pancake over and cook for another 1-2 minutes until the other side is also golden brown.
7. Remove the pancakes from the pan and set aside on a plate. Repeat in a few batches until until all the batter is used up.
8. Stack the pancakes and top with whipped cream, walnuts, and a drizzle of maple syrup.

Nutritional Value (Amount per Serving):

Calories: 110; Fat: 4.52; Carb: 14.14; Protein: 2.96

Hazelnut Olive Oil Shortbread

Prep Time: 10 Minutes   Cook Time: 20 Minutes   Serves: 18 To 24

Ingredients:

- 1 1/4 cups hazelnut meal
- 3/4 cup flour
- 1/4 cup brown sugar
- 1/4 cup powdered sugar, plus 1/4 cup for glaze
- 1 teaspoon kosher salt
- 1 lemon, zested and juiced
- 1 teaspoon vanilla
- 1/2 cup extra-virgin light olive oil

Directions:

1. Heat the oven to 375°F. Whisk together the hazelnut meal, flour granulated sugar, 1/4 cup powdered sugar, salt and lemon zest. Whisk in the vanilla and olive oil. The dough will be sandy and quite crumbly.
2. Press the dough firmly into a 8x8-inch (or 9x9-inch) dish. Bake for 20 minutes or until just lightly browned around the edges. Immediately cut the shortbread into diamonds or squares. Let cool completely before lifting them out of the pan, however.
3. Meanwhile, whisk together 1 tablespoon of the lemon juice and the remaining 1/4 cup powdered sugar and drizzle over the warm cookies.

Nutritional Value (Amount per Serving):

Calories: 102; Fat: 7.5; Carb: 7.67; Protein: 1.78

Rose Water Rice Pudding

Prep Time: 10 Minutes   Cook Time: 45 Minutes   Serves: 14

Ingredients:

- 4 cups water
- 2 cups uncooked long grain rice
- 4 cups half-and-half cream
- 1-1/2 cups sugar
- 1 to 2 teaspoons rose water
- Optional: Pomegranate seeds and chopped pistachios

Directions:

1. In a heavy saucepan, combine water and rice; bring to a boil over medium heat. Reduce heat; cover and simmer until water is absorbed, about 15 minutes. Add cream and sugar; bring to a boil. Reduce heat; simmer, uncovered, until slightly thickened, 30-40 minutes. Stir in rose water. Refrigerate until chilled, at least 2 hours. Stir in additional cream to reach desired consistency. If desired, top with pomegranate seeds and pistachios.

Nutritional Value (Amount per Serving):

Calories: 174; Fat: 1.94; Carb: 35.49; Protein: 4.16

Homemade Pita Bread

Prep Time: 25 Minutes   Cook Time: 5 Minutes   Serves: 1

Ingredients:

- 1 cup lukewarm water
- 2 teaspoons dry active yeast
- ½ teaspoon granulated sugar
- ½ cup whole wheat flour divided
- 2 cups all-purpose flour divided
- 1 teaspoon salt
- 2 tablespoons olive oil

Directions:

1. Add the water, yeast, and sugar to the bowl of a mixer and whisk until the yeast and sugar are dissolved. Stir in ¼ cup wheat flour and ¼ cup of all-purpose flour. Once combined, cover and set in a warm spot for 15 minutes or so. The mixture should become nice and bubbly, which is your sponge.
2. Stir in the remaining whole wheat flour, one ¼ cup of all-purpose flour (leaving ½ cup for dusting),salt, and olive oil. Mix until a shaggy dough forms. Dust lightly with flour and use the dough hook to knead in the bowl

for 1-2 minutes on low speed.

3. Dust a clean surface with a little flour and transfer the dough. Knead by hand for a few minutes until it becomes smooth. It should still be a little tacky, so be careful not to knead too much flour into it. Place in an oiled bowl and turn the dough to ensure it's covered with the oil. Cover the bowl with plastic wrap or a clean kitchen towel and set aside to rise until doubled in size, about an hour.

4. Punch down the dough and turn it out onto a floured surface. Divide it into eight equal portions and form them into balls. Cover and let the dough balls rest for 10-15 minutes.

5. Use a rolling pin to roll the balls out on a lightly floured surface until they are about 8-inches in diameter and roughly ¼ inch thick, and set aside until ready to cook.

6. Heat a large skillet over medium heat. Add a teaspoon or two of olive oil and use a clean kitchen towel or a paper towel to wipe the oil around the inside of the pan and soak up any excess oil. Place one rolled pita dough into the pan and cover with a lid for 30 seconds. Flip the pita over, cover, and cook for an additional 1.5-2 minutes. Fli, cover, and cook once more for about 1 minute.

7. Remove the cooked pita to a clean kitchen towel and cover while you cook the remaining pitas.

Nutritional Value (Amount per Serving):

Calories: 326; Fat: 7.89; Carb: 59.64; Protein: 19.5

APPENDIX RECIPE INDEX

Made in United States
Troutdale, OR
12/26/2023

16461774R00064